YOUTH MINISTRY THAT WORKS

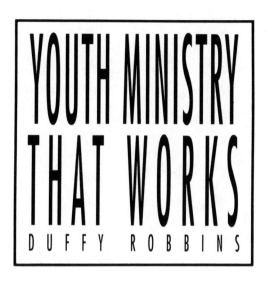

Portions of this book were previously published as
Programming to Build Disciples.

VICTOR BOOKS®

A DIVISION OF SCRIPTURE PRESS PUBLICATIONS INC.
USA CANADA ENGLAND

Unless otherwise noted, Scripture quotations are from *New American Standard Bible,* © the Lockman Foundation 1960, 1962, 1963, 1968, 1971, 1972, 1973, 1975, 1977. Other quotations are from the *Holy Bible, New International Version* (NIV), © 1973, 1978, 1984, International Bible Society, used by permission of Zondervan Bible Publishers; the *Revised Standard Version of the Bible* (RSV), © 1946, 1952, 1971, 1973; and the *Authorized King James Version* (KJV).

Library of Congress Cataloging-in-Publication Data

Robbins, Duffy.
   Youth ministry that works / by Duffy Robbins.
     p.   cm.
   Includes bibliographical references.
   ISBN 0-89693-918-9
   1. Church work with youth. 2. Discipling (Christianity)
I. Title.
BV4447.R638   1191
259′.23 — dc20   91-27850
                                                         CIP

---

   2   3   4   5   6   7   8   9   10   Printing/Year   95   94   93

To Maggie, my wife, friend, and
co-minister, and to Erin and Katie,
the two precious girls that God
has given us as our number-one
ministry of discipleship.

C O N T E N T S

A C K N O W L E D G M E N T S

This short book has actually been several years in the making. Through those years, there have been a number of people who have had a hand in its creation.

For that reason, I wish to thank J.L. and Patt Williams of the New Directions Evangelistic Association who originally built into me and my wife a vision for the ministry of multiplication.

Thanks to Robert Coleman, Trinity Evangelical Divinity School, whose writings sparked in me a desire to follow "The Master Plan of Evangelism."

I'm especially grateful to the youth groups of Barrington Baptist Church, Barrington, Rhode Island and the United Methodist Church of Wilmore, Kentucky. These folks gave me the great privilege of sharing their lives, and it was in that adventure that I had the chance to impart and sharpen my ministry of disciple-making. It was my experiences with these young disciples, and others like them, that built into me a strong commitment to minister with students.

My sincere thanks goes to our office staff, particularly Kim Feeser and Mary Noel Keough, without whom this manuscript would still be lost somewhere in the word processor. The Lord only knows what it's like to be secretary to both Tony Campolo and Duffy Robbins, and yet these women bear this cross with grace and humor. God bless them.

Duffy Robbins

A marksman firing with no target in sight will surely hit it. The tragedy is that all the shooting can be mistaken for accomplishment.

This is obvious in ministry with young people. Far too many workers expend energy running hither and yon, frantically trying to keep a program going, without any clear sense of direction. Activity may be equated with fulfillment.

The question has to be asked, "Where are we going?" Only then can we ascertain if what we are doing is worth the effort.

Duffy Robbins in this book honestly faces this basic issue. With keen insight and biblical realism, he sees beyond the necessity of getting attendance at youth meetings and comes to grips with the compelling mandate of Christ to make disciples. Recognizing that kids are at different stages of development, he analyzes their levels of receptivity to the Gospel claims and proposes ways to meet them. Through it all, the focus is on people, not mere programs.

The author writes out of years of experience as a youth leader in churches, and now as a college professor. There is a ring of credibility in his perception. Both as a practitioner and as a scholar he knows where ministry should lead, and in getting there he does not lose the reader in a smog of words. More to the point, he makes sense. This is the kind of book that gets the rubber down to the road. Those who have struggled with the task of equipping young men and women for fruitful Christian living will find it right on target.

Dr. Robert E. Coleman, Director
School of World Mission and Evangelism
Trinity Evangelical Divinity School

Lost on the Freeway

M aybe you've heard the story about the man and his wife riding down a busy freeway. Her complaints and grumbling come out at almost the same fast speed he is driving. After about 20 minutes, 25 miles, and 29 insults, this gentleman has had it. He loses it all and screams, "Will you stop nagging me? OK! You're right! We're lost! But, you gotta admit, we're making great time!"

Unfortunately, that is characteristic of the way a lot of folks approach youth ministry. We give more attention to distance and speed than to ultimate destination. It's no wonder that a lot of our youth programs are running out of gas. We're spending our money, our people, and our time trying to build good youth ministries, while in most cases we've given almost no thought to the two key questions: *Where are we now?* and *Where do we want to go?*

There are several different approaches to the "Lost-on-the-Freeway Syndrome." Probably the most common response is the one we see in the hapless, heavy-footed husband mentioned in the opening paragraph. Most of us are too busy to be bothered with questions about destination. "We've got some kids meeting in the church basement on Sunday nights. They're pretty regular. Something must be right. Let's not rock the boat!" As long as our programs are on the move, we would rather not be bothered with questions like, "Where are they moving to?"

A second type of response commonly seen in our youth ministries is this sort: "You're right, I think we are lost. Let's just keep on driving until we see something that will get us back on track." So we

13

spend more money, more time, and more people hoping we will stumble into the "right" direction, searching through each new promotional mailing, resource packet, or youth magazine article hoping that we will find just the right idea, just the right route, to get us back on the highway of "successful" youth ministry. Never mind that we've still no sense of destination or even our present location. More movement, more programs, and more money will surely get us back on track.

A third response that is all too common in our youth ministries is the kind exhibited by this statement: "Well, we can't be lost. Look at all the cars on this same freeway. If it's working for them, it ought to work for us. Let's just keep going." We don't stop to ask ourselves if we really want to go to the same destination as the others using this route. And, of course, there are many routes to the same destination, but the right route is the route that begins where you are!

Probably the most typical response of our local churches to the "Lost-on-the-Freeway Syndrome" is represented by a fourth statement: "You're right. We are lost. We don't know where we're going. We've got to do something drastic! Let's buy a new car!" So many churches who sense that their programs are aimless and ineffective decide for some reason that their best response to the situation is to either build a new building or shop around for a new program—a new idea book, a new curriculum, or a new magazine resource. But if a church is "lost on the freeway," buying a new car isn't going to solve the problem.

ONLY ONE SOLUTION

There is only one response that makes much sense when you are lost on the freeway. Only one response can keep us from driving aimlessly for an unknown, undetermined destination until we either run out of road, run out of gas, run out of drivers, or run out of kids who are willing to ride with us! We start by pulling over, turning off the engine, and taking a good long look at the map! This book is about you and your youth ministry. It is about honest evaluation of where your group is and where it should be heading. And it is about how you can get there.

If I had been reading this book in my early years of youth ministry, I would have read through that last paragraph and decided right away that the first two sections of this book could be ignored. "That's just philosophy, and what counts when you're working with kids is not what you think; it's what you do." Confident that my two years of vast experience had helped me to avoid wasting time I could be spending with kids, I would plunge straight ahead to the "ideas" section of the book. Looking for new exits and new routes, I wouldn't have taken the necessary time to ask myself where my program was and where was it headed.

There are a lot of reasons to avoid evaluation:

1. Evaluation takes time. That's a commodity that most youth workers don't have. "I don't have time to talk theory, man. I'm just trying to survive through Sunday night."
2. Evaluation is inconvenient. It may mean that we have to make some changes, and that always shakes up church people.
3. The embarrassing thing about defining a target is that we may finally discover that after all this time, we've been missing the mark. Personally, as a self-confessed William Tell, with a seminary degree and four years of youth ministry under my belt, I was not eager to hear that.

ON THE OTHER HAND . . .

I chuckled the first time a colleague in youth ministry said to me, "There's only one thing worse than driving a van load of junior-high kids to a bowling alley, staying there for two hours, and then driving them back to the church for an all-night lock-in (everybody knows better than to call them "*sleep*-overs"!). That is doing all of that once a month, and then going home tired on Saturday morning, sleeping through a potential Saturday with your family, and then waking up Saturday afternoon without really being sure *why* you had done it, or *what* you had actually accomplished."

I stopped chuckling after about two years of youth ministry.

On Friday nights, when I said good-bye to my wife and left my kids at home so I could spend the evening with somebody else's kids, I couldn't avoid asking myself what I was accomplishing with this activity. Where would it take me? I didn't chuckle very much when one of my ministry team members resigned because he "just wasn't motivated" to spend so much time with the kids when he couldn't see we were going anywhere.

Don't get me wrong. I loved the youth in our group. We had some super times and our group was getting bigger. The congregation was impressed, but deep down I knew: I was making great time, but I had no sense of where I was going.

15

"WITHOUT A VISION . . ."

Forced to reevaluate our program, I took a careful look at where we were. I surveyed our kids on a variety of issues. I read books, talked to colleagues, and prayed. And I began to realize something that has changed my ministry: If I hoped to work with kids for very long, I would have to be sustained by a vision that was bigger than Friday night's rock-a-thon, Sunday night's pizza party, and Tuesday night's skate-down (our kids were "holy rollers"). I needed a vision that was worth my life, my enthusiasm, and my energy. Without that vision, like some of my team members, and so many of my *ex*-youth minister friends, I knew I couldn't go the long haul.

Proverbs 29:18 reads, "Where there is no vision, the people perish" (KJV).

Another translation renders this verse: "Where there is no vision, the people are unrestrained" (NASB). By "pulling over" in my own ministry, I had a chance to go back to the map. There, in the Scriptures, I found a mandate for ministry that has given my years of youth work purpose, focus, and genuine vitality. Having a biblically defined destination, I was able to develop programs that would route my students and leaders in a direction that would help us reach our goals. In the pages that follow, I'm going to share that vision. It's really not a new idea. But I hope this book will provide some new strategies for making that vision a reality in your youth program. Maybe it will keep some of us from being lost on the freeway. I *can't* promise you'll *ever* develop a taste for junior-high lock-ins!

YOUTH MINISTRY
THAT WORKS

SECTION ONE

Ministry from the Inside Out

Being Who God Calls You to Be

was about two weeks into my first full-time youth ministry position when this sweet lady walked up to me after a Sunday morning service and handed me the following document entitled "Church Staff Job Descriptions." Parts of it (and I'm not saying which parts) were hauntingly accurate!

Church Staff Job Descriptions

PASTOR:
Able to leap tall buildings in a single bound;
is more powerful than a locomotive;
is faster than a speeding bullet;
walks on water;
gives policies to God.

ASSOCIATE PASTOR
Is able to leap short buildings in a single bound;
is as powerful as a switch engine;
is just as fast as a speeding bullet;
walks on water if the sea is calm;
talks with God.

EDUCATIONAL DIRECTOR:
Leaps short buildings with a running start;
is almost as powerful as a switch engine;
is faster than a speeding BB;

walks on water if he or she knows where the stumps are;
talks with God before and after most board meetings concerning the budget.

MUSIC DIRECTOR:
clears a quonset hut;
loses race with a locomotive;
can fire a speeding bullet;
swims well;
is occasionally addressed by God.

YOUTH DIRECTOR:
Runs into small buildings;
recognizes locomotives two out of three times;
used a squirt gun in college;
knows how to use the water fountain;
mumbles to himself.

CHURCH SECRETARY:
Lifts buildings to walk under them;
kicks locomotives off the track;
catches speeding bullets in her teeth;
freezes water with a speeding glance;
when God speaks she says, "May I ask who's calling?"

It's intriguing to consider some of the stereotypes that emerge when we think about people in ministry—particularly youth workers. Some of us envision "Mike Macho," this ruggedly handsome, robust, all-around athletic stud who sort of wins kids by the sheer strength of his natural abilities. He's the guy who beats the rest of the kids to the top of the mountain on the backpacking trip. He plays guitar like James Taylor, can bench press the entire junior high group, and sometimes, just for fun, catches frisbees in his teeth. My own observation is that these people never have names like Duffy either; it's always something like Buck Studd or Rocky Montana!

Then, of course, if you're a female it's quite a different stereotype altogether. The stereotypical youth ministry female is "Jane Joyful." She's just always "so bubbly" and "so lively;" she "just loves those kids." She always wears "neat" clothes and is "always in a good mood." Actually, it sort of makes you want to throw up.

In reality, if there's one thing I've learned in youth ministry over the last 20 years, it is that there is no set personality type or character profile that describes an effective youth worker. I think of Bob, a North Carolina pastor, who has been actively working with students since I was in junior high school. Or Jane, a married mother of three (two of whom are teenagers), who has developed a wonderful ministry as a youth volunteer with her group in Atlanta. There's David in Tennessee, whose behind-the-scenes style has been quietly nurturing teenage disciples in the same church for the last 7 years.

They are young. They are old. They are outgoing. They are quiet. They are everything from sports car to Jeep, L.L. Bean to K-Mart, Gatorade to Mello Yellow, Bill Cosby to Mr. Rogers. There simply is no perfect resumé for youthwork. God isn't looking for "cool" people; He's looking for "called" people.

SEEING WITH THE HEART
Far more important than any of these outward characteristics is the inward heart of the youth worker. That is where effective youth work begins. Before there is ever a vision, there must be a visionary—a person who sees not only with the eyes, but with the heart. Youth ministry presents its own unique kinds of challenges and opportunities. For a person whose heart is sensitive to those opportunities and challenges, the qualities that count are more inward in nature.

QUALITY ONE: DILIGENCE
"The one also who had received the two talents came up and said, 'Master, you entrusted to me two talents; see I have gained two more talents.' "

"His master said to him, 'Well done, good and faithful slave; you were faithful with a few things, I will put you in charge of many things; enter in to the joy of your master.' " (Matthew 25:22, 23)

There is perhaps no quality more important in a youth worker than diligence—being faithful to invest whatever gifts God has given us to maximize our impact for Him. We all know youth workers who seem to have an infinite number of talents, everything from the gift of "guitar-ness" to the gift of "funniness" the the gift of "cool appearance and facial hair." But Scripture and experience bear testimony to the fact that the number of talents is not nearly as important as our willingness to make diligent use of the talents we've been given.

In youth work, we have to overcome two major obstacles to make diligent use of our talents. The first is laziness. When the Master of Jesus' parable confronted the unfaithful slave in Matthew 25 (see verse 26), it wasn't because he had only one talent, or because he lacked any particular ability. The Master condemned him as a "wicked, *lazy* slave." Perhaps it was true that he was not as gifted as the other servants, but he should have made better use of the talent he had. He lacked diligence.

Close Enough for Horseshoes and Youth Work

One learns very early in youth work that youth ministry is one of those fields where we can be either incredibly energetic and creative, or woefully laid back and sloppy, and for the most part, very few people will notice the difference. It's remarkable how few youth workers ever enjoy serious, constructive accountability. Nobody seems to know (or care?) what we're doing until something drastic happens (e.g., a bus breaks down, the kitchen is left messy, a hymnbook is marred in the sanctuary, someone made a call to the "Nasty Talk" 900-line on the church phone).

If a youth worker doesn't have enough diligence to be a self-starter, it's quite possible that there will be no start at all. We're not talking here about either legalism or clock-watching; just earnest, responsible effort. For example, for a professional youth worker this might mean something as simple as keeping regular office hours. To be sure, our work with teenagers will mandate a schedule that stretches beyond "9–5." On the other hand, church secretaries and parents are often frustrated by our aloofness and unpredictability. I called a youth worker recently only to be told by his secretary, "We have no idea where he is; we never do. You might try Pizza Hut." It took an hour for my ear to thaw out.

For the volunteer, this diligent approach to ministry will be manifest in a desire to take the ministry seriously — to approach it with as much creativity and excellence as we might if it were our full time position. Actually, from a biblical standpoint, ministry *is* our full-time calling, whether we are paid for it or not. We simply can't afford to get in the habit of thinking, "Well, we could probably do more, but it'll be OK for teenagers. . . ."

At the same time, diligence is not the same as feverish activity. As one writer put it, "The Father bids us to do His business, not to fill our schedules with busy-ness." I have met lots of youth workers who are whirling dervishes of activity — even to the point of neglecting

24

their families and their own personal walk with God—but they seldom get anything of significance done. The key is not activity, but productivity. In his excellent book, *The Normal Christian Worker,* Watchman Nee puts it this way:

> It is not feverish activity of people whose restless dispositions keep them ever on the go that will meet the need, but the alertness of a diligent servant who has cultivated the upward gaze and can always see the Father's work that is waiting for his cooperation. . . . Jesus did not just come to make contacts with men; He came to seek them out and to save them. . . . Some Christian workers seem almost devoid of any sense of responsibility; they do not realize the vastness of the field; they do not feel the urge to reach the uttermost ends of the earth with the Gospel; they just do their little bit and hope for the best.

What Could I Possibly Do?

The other obstacle to diligence in youth ministry is intimidation, the feeling that we simply aren't cool enough, talented enough or young enough to impact a student's life for Christ. In the words of the unfaithful servant (Matthew 25:25), "I was afraid and went out and hid your talent in the ground. . . ."

One of the remarkable aspects of this parable is that Jesus spoke of no servant who had no talent. Nor did He in any sense belittle the fact that the one servant had only one talent while the other servants were better endowed. The issue was never how much talent the servants had; the issue was one of wisely investing whatever talents one has.

I believe there are very few people who simply are unable to do youth ministry. The tasks of youth work are diverse enough, and the kinds of students are so widely varied, I am convinced that most people can be effective with students if they are plugged into the right role with the right amount of support. For one thing, youth ministry allows us to use lots of wonderful talents that aren't recognized elsewhere: the ability to hang out and get close to students, the ability to tell stories, the ability to put biblical words to old sixties rock tunes, the ability to shoot Cheerios out of your nose! In youth ministry, there's a place for almost every talent.

On the other hand, I have seen many volunteer and professional youth workers through the years who either dropped out or burned out because they were constantly comparing their talents and abilities with the talents and abilities of other youth workers—never focusing on what they *could* do for the Master, but focusing rather on what they could *not* do. The diligent servant will accept the fact that God has uniquely and adequately gifted each of us for the ministry to which He has called us (1 Thessalonians 5:14, 24). Our response is faithful obedience and investment.

QUALITY TWO: STABILITY

"Therefore, my dear brothers, stand firm. Let nothing move you. Always give yourselves fully to the work of the Lord, because you know that your labor in the Lord is not in vain" (1 Corinthians 15:58).

I like to think of stability as nothing more than "stay-ability"—the ability to stay the course, the ability to stay with a work over the long haul, the ability to stay put when the going gets tough. It's a critical quality for those of us in youth ministry. It is the difference between a youth worker who blasts out of the gates for a quick sprint and one who works with kids over the long haul.

Youth work is not a ministry for the faint of heart. It's difficult. It takes us out of our comfort zones and leaves us feeling as if we've landed somewhere just south of the Twilight Zone. We seldom get clear affirmation or clear direction in our work. Quite often our ministry is marked more by sowing than by reaping. As one youth worker put it, "God has allowed me to be part of some wonderful success stories. Unfortunately, my involvement was usually in the opening chapters before the story really turned good!"

And yet, there is something about youth ministry that seems to attract people who are more oriented to "feelings," people who at the end of "E.T." were more apt to shed a tear at that touching scene of departure than to ask how some coat-hanger contraption could transmit signals into hyper-space. Maybe it's that ability to empathize and feel that makes us effective with kids.

But it can also make us fickle, susceptible to discouragement and self-doubt, characterized by vast mood swings that hinge not so much on the unshakable promises of God as on whether or not last night's youth group game bombed. Unfortunately, that kind of instability leads us to make bad decisions, snap judgments, and short-term choices. The biblical account of Peter gives us a classic glimpse into instability fleshed out.

Peter's trouble was not just superficial. There was a fundamental flaw in his character. He was governed by his emotions, and his conduct was always unpredictable, as is the conduct of people who are controlled by their feelings. The enthusiasm of such people carries them at times to the loftiest heights; at other times depression drives them into the depths. It is possible for such people to receive divine revelation, but it is also possible for them to put hindrances in the way of the divine purpose. . . .

Brothers and sisters, it is woefully possible that our fancied love for the Lord is little more than sentimental attachment. Our emotional reactions to his love are not necessarily so deep or so pure as we think. We feel we love him utterly, but we live so much in the feeling realm that we think we are the kind of people we feel we are. We feel we want to live for him alone and want to die for him if he so wills; but if the Lord does not shatter our self-confidence as he shattered Peter's, we shall go on being deceived by our feelings and life will be one of endless fluctuations. . . . The measure of our ability to follow the Lord is not assessed by the measure of our desire to follow him.

(*The Normal Christian Worker,* Watchman Nee)

QUALITY THREE: VISION

I recall very early in my ministry hearing this observation: "A task without a vision is nothing but drudgery; a vision without a task is nothing but dreaming; but a vision with a task is a missionary." It's a truth that touches the very heart of effective youth ministry. When asked, as often I am, what is the major principle that I would convey to someone just starting out in youth ministry, I find myself consistently probing for a vision: "What are you trying to accomplish? What is your vision? Make sure that you know what God has called you to do with students."

Vision is the absolute essential for someone who wants to stay fresh and enthusiastic about youth ministry over the long haul. It is the chief prevention for burn-out. I suspect that, most of the time, what we hear described as "burnout"—when people run out of steam—is more likely "blur-out"—when people are without a clear vision in ministry and simply don't have anything to get "steamed up" about!

27

Foresight and Insight

When we talk about a vision for youth ministry, we are speaking in one sense about a vision for plans — the ability to look ahead and see what God might want to accomplish. But we're talking about more than just foresight; we're talking about insight.

Dave Carver began his work in inner-city Pittsburgh with unusual optimism and expectancy. He dared to believe that God could raise up some new growth out of the burned-out stumps of inner-city blight. His vision was contagious. He started getting students excited, and then their parents, and then other people around the neighborhood.

Before long, Dave was offered a chance to reclaim and renovate an old abandoned movie theatre in the neighborhood. The place didn't look like much. It reeked from the garbage of neglect, vandals, drug users, and homeless people seeking shelter. What most people saw as a time capsule of dust, garbage, and destruction, Dave saw as a potential drop-in center and ministry headquarters.

Finally, over the course of several months, Dave had mobilized those kids and that neighborhood to make that vision a reality. To this day, there stands in a Pittsburgh neighborhood a completely renovated movie theater/youth activity center. It happened because one youth minister dared to dream big dreams for God. That's vision.

Seeing Beyond the Bloopers, Bungles, and Burps

But vision is more than seeing what God can do with mortar and drywall. Effective youth ministries are stoked by men and women who have a vision for what God can do with real flesh and blood — the kind of youth worker who can hear a kid sitting in the back of a van reciting the alphabet through a burp, and still believe that this same kid may one day be a missionary on a distant continent sharing his faith in an equally amazing way.

It is not naiveté or fluffy optimism. It is the kind of Christ-centered realism that can look at the dust and decay of an abandoned kid and trust in God's transforming power, which took the Peter of the Gospels (brash, impulsive, inconsistent, and timid about his faith) and molded him into the Peter of Acts (faithful, bold, and outspoken). It is realism rooted, first of all, in a biblical appraisal of who God is, and, second, in a fair-minded recollection of what God has done in our own lives through the years. Without this vision for what God can do in the lives of our students, we will be kicking Peters off of the youth

28

council because of one night's denial (John 18:15-27), or sending home a John Mark because of one instance of timidity (Acts 13:13; 15:15; 39).

My friend Jack has that kind of vision. As a youth pastor, he was willing to take some risks with a young college intern named Derek. At first, it didn't look like a very promising wager. Derek's attitude wasn't that great. He had a knack for saying the wrong thing at the wrong time, and he cultivated a generally sloppy personal appearance that made it hard for people to see beyond the externals.

I have to admit, as Derek's college professor, I wasn't very hopeful either. When Jack accepted Derek on his ministry team, my response was along the lines of, "Well, if you're really sure." I fully expected the arrangement to last no more than a few months. And, to be honest, there were several times when it seemed that projection might even have been optimistic. Jack would occasionally call my office, exasperated, giving me another "Derek story."

And yet, the amazing thing is that every time Derek was corrected he would respond. No matter how often he was taken down by rebuke, he always came back for more. Slowly but surely, miraculously and painstakingly, Derek began to change. Jack discovered that Derek had a remarkable gift of service. He could be given a task and, no matter how small, he would get it done. Plus, the guy turned out to be a computer genius. He reprogrammed and de-bugged every computer in the church. And he began to show an ability to draw close to students.

It's been about two years now, and Derek is a valued member of Jack's ministry team. He is well-respected and appreciated, and he's learning the ropes so that someday he can begin his own youth ministry. His story is a story of vision — the story of how one youth minister dared to take a chance on a student, looking beyond the negatives to see the positives that only God could see.

QUALITY FOUR: INTEGRITY

Yet another Christian leader had fallen. It was obvious that the interviewer could scarcely believe himself that he was asking these questions to this renowned and respected pastor. And yet, he pressed on with painful probing:

Interviewer: "You have said there is no excuse for what you have done. In addition, you have insisted that sin be called sin. What factors contributed to the adultery?"

Christian Leader: " . . . It was a number of things. From about 1982 on I was desperately weary in spirit and in body. I was working harder and enjoying it less.

"Satan's ability to distort the heart and the mind is beyond belief. I assume the responsibility for what I did; I made those decisions out of a distorted heart.

"In addition, I now realize I was lacking in mutual accountability through personal relationships. We need friendships where one man regularly looks another man in the eye and asks hard questions about our moral life, our lust, our ambitions, our ego." (*Christianity Today,* "A Talk with the MacDonalds," July 10, 1987)

Integrity comes from the root word *integrate,* the ability to take various parts and knit them together into a unified whole. It is vital for youth ministry leadership. We are people with myriad constituencies. Through the course of our week, we walk into and out of a number of situations, each of them bringing its own set of expectations, obligations, and responsibilities.

The average youth worker is trying to balance commitments to his or her spouse, children, ministry, personal relationship with God, and (perhaps) a full-time job other than youth work. The list goes on and on. Integrating each of these commitments into a unified whole is the constant challenge of people in ministry. It's not easy. So often what appears to be an adequate amount of attention to one area means we have to neglect another area.

I remember as a little boy watching this amazing character on "Captain Kangaroo." He ran around the studio trying to keep about 30 plates simultaneously spinning on top of sticks. With music blaring he would race from one wobbling plate to another, every now and then having to suffer the loss of a neglected plate that stopped its spinning and crashed to the floor.

I've seen youth ministers whose lifestyle suggests this same harried and hurried juggling act. No wonder that we become weary "in spirit and in body," and find ourselves "working harder and enjoying it less." Integrity is integrating all that we are and all that we do into a consistent pattern of living.

First Things First

It begins with an absolute bedrock commitment to maintain intimacy with God. The greatest danger in youth ministry is that we become so enamoured with the calling that we begin to neglect the Caller.

We are so immersed in doing Christian work that we tend to mistake "doing" with "being and growing."

> Beware of any work for God which enables you to avoid concentration on Him. A great many Christian workers worship their work. Jesus told the disciples not to rejoice in successful service, and yet this seems to be the one thing in which most of us do rejoice. One life wholly devoted to God is of more value to God than one hundred lives simply awakened by His Spirit. . . . So often we mar God's designed influence through us by our self-conscious effort to be consistent and useful. Jesus says there is only one way to develop spiritually, and that is by concentration on God.
>
> (*My Utmost for His Highest,* Oswald Chambers)

My very first priority is to claim new ground in my relationship with God. And yet, it's ironic: that is the area of my life that people actually know least about. It is private and, to some extent, solitary. Which is, of course, the reason that I can so easily neglect it without being found out. As long as the ministry is moving along and I don't tip my hand, I could be dry as a bone spiritually without anyone knowing it.

It is woefully easy in youth ministry to find ourselves doing what I call "third person reading"—reading through a devotional, not for what God might say *to* us, but for what God might say *through* us to our students. We begin to discover that more and more of our Bible reading is in preparation for a talk or a study rather than for our own devotional refreshment.

Before we ever crack that youth ministry resource book, or read one more page of "how to have an incredible youth ministry," we had better return to the source of our power. Barry St. Clair once told a story about a highway department worker who was busily painting lines down the middle of the highway. When his foreman inspected the work, he was unhappy to find that the middle lines were getting progressively fainter every few yards, till finally they could hardly be seen at all. When the foreman confronted the worker with his concern, the worker replied, "I can't help it. I'm trying, but I keep getting farther and farther away from the bucket."

We probably don't need another book that talks about how to get paint from the bucket. For those who are hungry, the bookstore cupboards are far from bare. What we may need is a reminder that any youth worker who wants to paint solid lines of ministry that go the distance had better develop the discipline of bringing the bucket with him. God must be the first priority of our schedule. Integrity begins with a commitment to stay close to the Source.

Maintaining a Healthy Life Beyond the Church

I had been at the National Youthworker Convention for three days, and for each day I had been at the convention I had heard another story about someone in youth ministry whose marriage was falling apart. Here were six people who obviously, at one point, had been very much in love with their spouses. But because of the demands of ministry, they had left the fire untended long enough that the coals of the relationship had virtually burned out. It is no longer an uncommon story.

In one of the earliest editions of the *Wittenburg Door,* I read the following article. I read it at least once a year, and I never fail to be chilled by its warning.

My husband is a full time youth director. He is extremely dedicated and spends between fifty to seventy hours a week with young people.

I think the reason he is so successful with kids is that he is always available to them, always ready to help when they need him.

That may be the reason why the attendance has more than doubled in the past year. He really knows how to talk their language. This past year he would be out two and three nights a week talking with kids until midnight. He's always taking them to camps and ski-trips and overnight camp-outs. If he isn't with the kids, he's thinking about them and preparing for his next encounter with them.

And if he has any time left after that, he is speaking or

attending a conference where he can share with others what God is doing through him. When it comes to youth work, my husband has always been one hundred per cent.

I guess that's why I left him.

There isn't much left after one hundred per cent.

Frankly, I just couldn't compete with "God." I say that because my husband always had a way of reminding me that this was God's work and he must minister where and when God called him. Young people desperately needed help and God had called him to help them. When a young person needed him, he had to respond or he would be letting God and the young person down.

When I *did* ask my husband to spend some time with the kids or me, it was always tentative and if I became pushy about it I was "nagging," "trying to get him out of God's work," "behaving selfishly," or I was "revealing a spiritual problem."

Honestly, I have never wanted anything but God's will for my husband, but I never could get him to consider that maybe his family was part of that will.

It didn't matter how many "discussions" we had about his schedule, he would always end with, "OK, I'll get out of the ministry, if that's what you want." Of course I didn't want that, so we would continue as always until another "discussion."

You can only ask for so long. There is a limit to how long you can be ignored and put off. You threaten to leave without meaning it until you keep the threat. You consider all the unpleasant consequences until they don't seem unpleasant anymore. You decide that nothing could be more unpleasant than being alone, feeling worthless.

You finally make up your mind that you are a person with real worth as an individual. You assert your ego and join womanhood again.

That's what I did.

I wanted to be more than a housekeeper, diaper changer, and sex partner.

I wanted to be free from the deep bitterness and guilt that slowly ate at my spiritual and psychological sanity.

Deep inside there was something making me not only dislike my husband, but everything he did or touched.

His "I love you" became meaningless to me because he

didn't act like it. His gifts were evidence to me of his guilt because he didn't spend more time with me. His sexual advances were met with a frigidity that frustrated both of us and deepened the gap between us.

All I wanted was to feel as though he really wanted to be with me. But no matter how hard he tried, I always felt like I was keeping him from something. He had a way of making me feel guilty because I had forced him to spend his valuable time with the kids and myself.

Just once I wish he would have canceled something for us instead of canceling us.

You don't have to believe this, but I really loved him and his ministry once. I never wanted him to work an eight to five job. Nor did I expect him to be home every night. I tried to believe every promise he made me, honestly hoping things would change, but they never did.

All of a sudden I woke up one day and realized that I had become a terribly bitter person. I not only resented my husband and his work, but I was beginning to despise myself. In desperation to save myself, our children, and I guess, even my husband and his ministry, I left him.

I don't think he really believed I'd leave him. I guess I never really believed I'd leave him either.

But I did.

(*Wittenburg Door,* "Diary of a Mad Housewife," June, 1971)

WHY DOES IT HAPPEN?

Why is it that people who are otherwise compassionate, caring, sincere Christians walk away from a life-long vow? Here are people who would give their left arm to help a hurting teenager, and their right arm to help a couple going through a rough time. People who seem to have endless energy for spending time with others. Gifted communicators when speaking to a roomful of adolescents, seemingly so skilled in interpersonal relationships, and yet they are unable to hold together this most special and basic of all their relationships. How can that happen?

To be honest, I don't know.

I don't have any easy answers. But, I do know that there are several factors in youth work that bring extra strain to a family relationship:

1. Family life is not in the job description. To begin with, we are usually not rewarded or affirmed for spending time with our families. We are affirmed for spending extra nights out, "always being there" when someone needs us, and "being a team player," even if it means forfeiting family plans to do so.

2. Family life is not as easy as youth ministry. To be frank, it's much easier for me to be a good youth worker than it is to be a good father and a good husband. I can give the youth group kids all kinds of counsel about all kinds of topics, but when the situation turns dirty, I have the option of walking away from the problem. I can plead that the situation has grown beyond my expertise or responsibility. Not so with my family.

It's always easier to work through other people's problems than it is to work through my own. It's sort of like the old maxim: Minor surgery is when they operate on you; major surgery is when they operate on me.

3. Family problems aren't always so easily resolved. If push comes to shove, I could just tell a problem student that he's not allowed to come to youth group for a while. It's a bit more awkward to tell your child she can't come to dinner for the next three weeks.

Sometimes with a youth group student, when all else seems to be failing, I, at least, have the consolation that sooner or later this kid is going to graduate from the youth program. It may take a few years, but there is light at the end of the tunnel. Marriage doesn't offer us that easy out. We've got to work through the problems. We can't just wait for our spouse to "graduate" and move on.

Even if things turn nasty in the youth group, I know that I have six days to recuperate before the next round on Sunday night. Family living doesn't offer us that kind of breather. The problem that you left behind when you drove to the church on Sunday afternoon is going to be waiting right there when you come back through that door on Sunday night.

4. Family life doesn't always stroke the ego like youth group does. I've met youth workers who are deemed courageous and sacrificial because of the great amount of time they spend with their students. And that's great. But I'm not so sure how sacrificial it is. Back home at my house, there are diapers to be changed. Most of my students at youth group don't make those kinds of demands. There's garbage to be taken out at home, and toilets to be unclogged. We have custodians who do that stuff at church.

I'm not sure it's all that sacrificial to hang around good-looking teenage girls who look up to me and tell me it's been a wonderful night. When I do a great talk at youth group the students applaud and tell me how great I am. When I do that same talk at home people have a way of expecting me to live up to my words. That's not quite as invigorating.

5. Youth ministry just naturally entails unique demands on our time. If we want to spend time with teenagers, we must do it after school or on weekends. We can't as easily work their schedule around a normal workday schedule or a normal family schedule. They need our time, and the only hours of the day when we can meet that need is during what might have been prime time for the family.

6. Youth ministry requires us to straddle two cultures and two roles with very different demands. It's not so easy to walk back and forth between two different cultures everyday. The culture of teenagers and the culture of adulthood are quite different. They are rare youth ministers who can stop being "on" when they walk through the door of their own homes. I've met more than a few youth ministers who couldn't seem to stop being youth ministers long enough to be husbands and dads. All of a sudden, right in the middle of a long-needed family discussion over dinner, they are play-ing with the children and balancing a spoon on their nose!

GUARDING THE FAMILY

There are more than enough books about how to have a healthy family and a successful marriage. That isn't our purpose here. But the following questions might help those of us in youth ministry to maintain integrity in our family relationships.

1. Am I taking a day off and "keeping it holy"? I am told that my mentor and friend David Seamands once told a class of his at Asbury Seminary that what impressed him more than anything else from the four years of co-ministry we shared at the United Methodist in Wilmore, Kentucky was my unerring commitment to take a day off every week without fail. No cheating. No bringing work home. No phone calls. Just undivided attention to family for 24 hours.

God made the world and held things together for several thousand years before he had the benefit of our help. We need to understand that he can maintain this solo performance for at least one day a week without our assistance, and that there will be no serious dam-age to the Kingdom.

2. Who am I holding responsible for my family's schedule?
When the deal goes down, no one is responsible for our families but us. We can blame the elders, the students, the pastor. But when it's all said and done, my family is my responsibility before God.

For the most part, the average congregation will blindly affirm the youth minister who is out away from home eight nights a week. "What a commitment!" "What a great youth minister!" "What a zeal for youth ministry!" Until finally all of those nights away from home add up to a broken marriage. Then that same congregation will be saying, "What? A divorce? We're sorry, but we can't really allow a divorced person to serve on our staff."

It's not that anyone means wrong. It's just that we should not assume someone else is watching out for the welfare of our family. That is no one's responsibility but our own.

3. What am I doing to let my family members know that they are as special as the students in my youth program? Some of us go to great pains to show youth group kids how special they are. We send birthday cards and short notes. We attend athletic events and music recitals. We take them to meals and go to movies together.

But at the same time, we forget those birthday and anniversary dates so important in our own family. Or we're so busy watching the high school soccer team practice that we don't have time to go to our son's third grade play. It's true our families may understand and forgive us for these oversights — but should they have to? When was the last time you sent a short note to your spouse or your child just to tell them "how special" they are?

4. Do I invest as much creative effort to make my family a fun and special place as I invest in the youth group at church? Or has home become humdrum? We have to make youth group attractive or kids won't come. What are the consequences of an unattractive home life on our own children?

5. Am I giving my students a biblical model of a healthy marriage and effective parenting? A tragically high number of teenagers will never get an up-close picture of healthy family. It may well be that the closest they ever come to one is in our living rooms. Far more convincing than any Bible study or talk about the biblical guidelines for love and sexuality is a youth worker and spouse who are transparently and passionately in love with each other.

To watch a lot of youth workers one might suppose that our goal is to model how one can be a cool teenager. On the contrary, what they desperately need is for us to model fulfilled, contented adulthood—a mom who enjoys being a mom, a wife who enjoys being a wife. Most teenagers don't believe there is life or passion after the age of 20. A healthy model can teach them both.

PERSONAL MORALITY

Bill Hybels has defined integrity as being true to our beliefs even when no one is watching us. His point is well-taken. In a random survey of just over 200 youth workers, five basic areas of temptation and struggle emerged:

1. Sex (sexual temptation, lust, "impure thought life," pornography, masturbation, sexual misconduct)

2. Money (compromising integrity to get more, materialism, the problem of "low pay," "pilfering" church things, copyright violations, gambling)

3. Time (the abuse and misuse of time, loafing, laziness, neglect of family, neglect of job)

4. Success (competition in ministry, playing the "numbers game," pride, motivation for ministry)

5. Honesty (lying, "stretching the truth," taking credit for other people's ideas, honesty in counseling, keeping confidences, gossip)

Whether we are talking about questions of money or lust or untruthfulness, youth ministers face more than enough of the kind of ethical questions that can cripple or kill an effective ministry. Integrity is integrating what we say we believe into our everyday behavior.

Again, the purpose here is not to rewrite the book on personal integrity. It's all been written. On the other hand, 20 years of youth ministry have given me ample opportunity to learn some important principles about personal integrity in youth ministry.

Money and the Opposite Sex

I once heard Billy Graham tell a group of pastors that the two major pitfalls in ministry are money and the opposite sex. There are countless witnesses who bear unfortunate testimony to his words. Most falls don't begin with an intentional jump. They begin with someone getting carelessly close to the edge. We must be careful to avoid perilous counseling situations or financial arrangements that leave us vulnerable to a fall. Common sense and caution are the two basic rules.

It Could Happen to Us

The gravest danger upon hearing of someone else's failure is to think, "It could never happen to me." It's that kind of arrogance that lulls us off our guard and makes us prey to the roaring lion that prowls about. The day we begin thinking we have grown above temptation or matured beyond it, that is the day we move one giant step closer to the edge. In the words of E. Stanley Jones, we must be "eternally vigilant."

Don't Believe Everything You're Told

One of the reasons that we in youth ministry are so vulnerable to arrogance and temptation is that we spend most of our time around teenagers who think we are just a notch below superhuman. They hear our stories and believe every word of them. They see us two or three nights a week for a few hours when we are consciously at our best, and on the basis of that assume that we totally have it all together. Teenagers seldom confront us about our personal walk, our temptations, our family life, or our weak spots. It is quite easy for their shallow praise to drown out the voice of more mature discernment.

MORALITY ISN'T ALWAYS ENOUGH

What you may do and what you should do are often two different things. Archibald Hart, dean of the Fuller Graduate School of Psychology, points out one of the most slippery spots on the road of maintaining integrity:

> It's a strange paradox in Christian ministry: we can be super-sensitive to sin and immoral behaviors, but we are often oblivious to the need for ethical boundaries. This partially accounts for the fall of upright, spiritual, and well-intentioned pastors [and youth pastors]. Christian leaders can be so preoccupied with discerning whether something is sinful that they ignore the trickier question: Is this action a stepping stone to sin, even though it may not be sin in and of itself?
>
> This is why morality isn't always enough.
>
> ("Being Moral Isn't Always Enough,"
> Archibald D. Hart, *Leadership*, Spring, 1988)

Hart suggests these basic ethical principles:

1. The Principle of Accountability. Make sure that you are not a law unto yourself. In matters of finance and counseling, and perhaps in other areas where you feel temptation, seek out a small group of peers or a church committee to whom you will report and be held accountable, *whether they ask for it or not.* Often in youth ministry, they will not. Generally you will be given more than enough rope to hang yourself. Before you fall through the gallows, give a small group of people the authority to cut your rope!

2. The Principle of Confidentiality. In matters of counseling, our primary responsibility is to the teenager we are counseling. When once we pledge confidentiality to them, we are obliged to maintain it. The key here is to make sure that we do not promise something we cannot deliver.

If a student says to me, "I'm going to tell you something, but I've got to trust that you aren't going to tell anybody," my response is clear: "You may or may not choose to tell me this information. You can trust me to act in what I sincerely feel is your best interest. If that means I need to share your story, you can trust me to do that. If you are still willing to talk with me on those terms, I want very much to help you."

3. The Principle of Integrity. This last ethical principle suggested by Hart essentially sets some boundaries related to honesty. Before we do something, we need to be asking ourselves about honest motives. For example: Am I hosting this event to compete with the youth group down the street or am I doing it to reach new kids? Am I manipulating kids by the way I've used this music or this movie? Am I spending time with this student because I really want to help this student, or because her dad is the Chairman of the Deacon Board? Am I talking to these students because I can minister to them, or is it because they are the popular kids in the school and it makes me feel good to be seen with them?

NEVER WALK ALONE

The greatest single help in my own spiritual walk—apart from the guidance of my wife and the ministry of the Holy Spirit—has been a small circle of colleagues and friends that have known me for many years. These are people with whom I am in frequent contact, and with whom I feel I can be very honest and open. We all need some small group like this that the Spirit can use to be watchdogs of our souls.

41

SECTION TWO
A Vision for Student Discipleship

A Ministry Become Flesh

Several years ago, a Korean artist (a refugee from North Korea to South Korea) completed a remarkable piece of art depicting the standing figure of Jesus with arms outstretched. Surrounding the figure of Jesus around the border of the picture are 27 angels symbolizing the 27 books of the New Testament. Even if it had been a traditional painting, it would be an amazing work of art.

But what makes this piece even more incredible is that this Korean's artistry didn't come through sketchwork or drawing or brushstrokes, but through writing out the entire New Testament with a fine-point pen, shading various letters and words so that the images of Jesus and the angels would appear on the scroll. In other words, the figure of Jesus is not superimposed over the text of Scripture; it is actually the words themselves! It took the artist two years to write out the entire 185,000-plus words of the New Testament, shading each letter in just such a way that the detailed portrayal of Jesus and the angels would be clearly visible on his six-by-four-foot scroll.

In his devotional book, *The Word Became Flesh* (Abingdon Press, New York), E. Stanley Jones observes that the artist, through his painstaking and meticulous work, is giving us a powerful testimony to the miracle of "incarnation." It's a word that literally means "in flesh." Significantly, John's original usage of the phrase in John 1:14 is followed by this explanation: "Jesus dwelt among us." Literally, the phrase could be translated, "He pitched his tent among us." In this short phrase we are seeing, all at once, the genius, the wonder, and the mystery of the Gospel. Jesus was Immanuel, "God with us."

MINISTRY BECOME FLESH

Somewhere between the sketches of that old drawing and the words of this familiar passage is a truth that takes us right to the heart of the ministry of discipling teenagers. The central challenge of youth ministry is to be incarnational — to flesh out the Word of God to the students with whom we are working, to consistently, creatively, and obediently live out the Word of God in their presence. Paul put it this way:

> Your attitude should be the same as that of Christ Jesus: Who, being in very nature God, did not count equality with God something to be grasped, but made Himself nothing, taking the very nature of a servant, being made in human likeness. And being found in appearance as a man, He humbled Himself and became obedient to death — even death on a cross!
>
> (Philippians 2:5-8)

As one writer comments, this is theology that includes geography. It points us to a youth ministry that reaches beyond the safe walls of a youth room plastered with Christian posters, and basically challenges us to be *"among"* kids, on their turf, on their terms. Sad to say, for too many of us our style has been more along the lines of the "Bo Peep" approach: "Leave them alone and they'll come home, wagging their tails behind them." We've stayed back at the church and waited for the kids to flock to our meetings. Unfortunately, as anyone who has worked very much with teenagers knows, Bo "don't know diddley" about youth ministry. In fact, what more often happens is that teenagers wander off and wind up lost in pursuit of a hundred different shepherds.

INCARNATIONAL YOUTH MINISTRY

Youth ministry expert Jeff Johnson tells the story of a high school counselor named Mary:

> She seemed unable to reach a certain group of girls at her high school and in deep frustration finally asked one of the girls what the problem was. The girl blurted out, "Well, just look where you are!" Mary was sitting behind her desk in the air-

conditioned office, across the hall from the Dean of Women where these girls regularly visited for disciplinary reasons. So Mary did some research and discovered that this group hung out around the cafeteria door that led to the parking lot. It was hot and unpleasant, but being near the boiler room, they could smoke and skip classes easily.

Over the summer, Mary moved her office . . . to the boiler room! She had to work through all sorts of red tape with her principal and school board members who assured her it was very unprofessional, but she did it. Relationships started clicking as kids realized she was serious about being their friend. Her nickname soon become "Moms," even though she was the same concerned person as before. All that had changed was geography, but it convinced those girls that she would do what was necessary to have a relationship with them.

That's a good picture of incarnational youth ministry. You can almost hear Paul writing, "Though being in very nature faculty, she did not consider air-conditioning something to be grasped . . . but humbled herself even to the level of the boiler room!"

CLAIMING HOLY GROUND

If we hope to shape youth ministries that are incarnational, the first question we must ask ourselves is, "Where are our students?" It stands to reason that if we want to develop a ministry that goes where kids are and dwells among them, we better do some serious thinking about where kids are.

Art Erickson, veteran youth worker from Park Avenue United Methodist Church in Minneapolis, refers to this question/ investigation process as "exegeting a community." It doesn't have to be a computer-based research project. It is the kind of amateur sociological research that entails such scientific methods as driving around on Friday nights, talking to kids, and trying to get a feel for what is happening with teenagers in the community.

Mary found out about the kids in her school by simply keeping her eyes and ears open. The students themselves are usually the best source of information, but there are others: school counselors, parents, fellow youth workers. Sometimes the most effective first-hand research of the teenage world is going to a football game or volunteering to chaperone at a school dance.

The crucial questions we want to ask are these:

1. Where are the students in our community? For some communities, the big Friday night sport is cruising. In other communities, kids spend all their time at the beach. In still other communities, a majority of the teenagers spend their time sitting in front of a convenience store or hanging out in a mall. For others, most of the action takes place at school sports events. Where is the "boiler room" in your community?

2. What are the various groupings among teenagers in our community? The average high school might have anything from jocks to nerds to skaters to zipperheads to dexters to band freaks to druggies. It doesn't take many hours in the school cafeteria before it becomes apparent that each sub-group has its own closed society with its own set of standards and behaviors. The party animals are in their corner of the cafeteria chugging milk cartons; the jocks are over in their section pumping tables; the band freaks are in their corner talking clarinets; and then there are the head-bangers who are sort of off in their area, and they aren't saying anything because they can't hear anyway!

Canadian youth worker and researcher Donald Posterski reminds us that these groups have very little "cross-pollination." Unlike the youth ministry of the fifties and sixties, it is no longer a matter of reaching "key kids" whose popularity wins us an audience with less popular students. If we are really serious about reaching those students, the key will be to develop relationships which penetrate each of these small "friendship clusters" — "pitching our tent among them." To do that effectively, we need to understand who these groups are.

3. What "boundaries" are we working with in our ministry? Are we targeting one particular group? One particular sex? One specific age group? One specific high school or middle school?

4. What are some of the socio-economic realities of our community? Is this a rural environment, or is it urban, or suburban? What kinds of families live in our area? How many of our students are from single-parent families? Blended families? What is the median income? What are the major kinds of employment? A lot of the hard data is available through a township office, or from the local planning commission. We can probably get a sense of the big picture by simply keeping our eyes and ears open, and being sensitive to these kinds of issues.

48

5. What kind of agencies are already at work in our community? What are the needs that we can meet? With which agencies might we be able to network to better serve the community without duplicating efforts? What other youth ministries are serving this area?

DWELLING AMONG THEM

When I first began doing youth work, I was working as an intern with a para-church mission whose primary vision and focus was to reach out to nonchurched high school students. I spent many a lunch hour walking (and sometimes stalking) a campus trying to develop relationships with students who not only didn't know me, but apparently didn't often feel any great desire to know me. It was some of my scariest youth ministry.

Will they wonder why I'm here on their campus? They know I'm not a student. They know I'm not a faculty or staff person. They know I'm not a parent. That only leaves narcotics officer, sex criminal, or axe murderer. It was a genuine cross-cultural outreach and I wasn't at all sure how the natives of this culture were going to respond.

As I continued to spend time with students, though, one truth came back to me over and over again: Kids are open to, and will find time for, genuine, sincere love. It will not be easy for most of us. To begin with, the students are skeptical. They aren't exactly used to having adults seek them out for the purpose of friendship. More often than not, in a high schooler's world, if "Mr. So-and-So wants to see you," it is not because he craves your fellowship!

The biggest mistake is to become intimidated. For the normal adult, spending time on a high school campus or at a junior high sports event conjures up feelings of expectancy and excitement that rank somewhere between oral surgery and a tax audit. But spending time with students—"contact work" as it's often called—doesn't have to be a cross between pulling teeth and paying taxes. Here are some simple guidelines to remember:

1. You cannot build an in-depth relationship with every student on every campus in your community. Particularly if you are a volunteer youth worker, you will need to focus your time on building relationships with a few students. No matter how much compassion we have, it's impossible to hug a group of 30 people. They must be embraced one at a time.

One youth leader can influence only a limited number of students.

The genius of team ministry is that co-workers can take the time to build real friendships with individual students instead of trying to befriend a mob.

2. Contact work is not about "acting like a teenager." There's nothing more pitiful than a 40-year-old woman standing around a group of teenagers going, "Whoa, dudes, what it is! Giddown wit' yo' bad foot." Puuulllease!! The key to contact work is not acting like a teenager. The key to contact work is being comfortable around teenagers when *they* act like teenagers.

3. Don't be threatened because you seem to be able to relate to some students better than others. That's normal. Some people relate better to students who are into athletics. Others relate better to kids who are into computers. I, personally, relate better to kids who are into premature hairloss. This is nothing to feel weird about. Again, that's why a team of leaders can embrace more kids than the lone ranger of youth ministry.

I have a youth worker friend named Bill who often points back to one man in his church who was a significant spiritual influence during his teenage years. This guy was kind of a classic nerd, plastic deal in his shirt pocket with lots of different pens and mechanical pencils, always accompanied by a monstrous clump of keys hanging from his belt. Not exactly the essence of cool! But this man was in charge of audio-visual equipment in the congregation, and he often recruited one or two youth group kids to help him in his work.

It probably didn't seem like much at the time, but this man befriended Bill. He made Bill feel important, showed him that he could make a contribution to the church. And today Bill is a committed Christian and active in ministry, due in part to the influence of this one man. Now, granted, this is not the kind of guy who is going to impact every teenager. But no one needs to be. Incarnational ministry is getting close to a *few* students and loving them into a relationship with Christ.

4. Every conversation does not have to be an in-depth proclamation of the Gospel. The freedom of incarnational ministry is that we are *living* out our message, fleshing out the Word in the presence of students. That means that I will sometimes spend an afternoon with a group of guys and never once directly mention Jesus, sin, the Trinity, or hypostatic union.

Sure, there will be times when we will talk specifically about spiritual matters. But we needn't feel that we've betrayed our calling or lost an opportunity because we haven't cited at least seven biblical passages. Talking with students about their life, their concerns, their areas of interest — that may be the kind of vital ministry that prepares the ground for later sowing of the seed. Of his own incarnational style, Paul wrote, "We loved you so much that we were delighted to share with you not only the Gospel of God but our lives as well, because you had become so dear to us" (1 Thessalonians 2:8).

5. Our witness should be based more on the signpost model and less on the salesman model. The difference between the two is basic: signposts point the way; salesmen try to close the deal. Incarnational youth ministry is very similar to what Moses talks about in his charge to parents.

> Love the Lord your God with all your heart and with all your soul and with all your strength. These commandments that I give you today are to be upon your hearts. Impress them on your children. Talk about them when you sit at home and when you walk along the road, when you lie down and when you get up. Tie them as symbols on your hands and bind them on your foreheads.
>
> (Deuteronomy 6:5-8)

Too often our youth ministry is limited to a Sunday School lesson or a special devotional talk at youth group. In fact, one of the basic principles at the heart of incarnational ministry is that God often works better between lessons, after the study is over, when the van has long since left the church parking lot and we're taking kids home!

Isn't it intriguing to read the words of those disciples on the road to Emmaus (Luke 24:13-33)? "They asked each other, 'Were not our hearts burning within us while He talked with us on the road and opened the Scriptures to us?' " One of the hallmarks of Jesus' ministry is that His style of witness was not some canned, rehearsed sales pitch. It was a consistent lifestyle of living out and talking about the Kingdom of God. Much of the time, Jesus' greatest work was done "on the road," in transit while he was walking with His disciples or boating with His disciples or praying with His disciples.

That's a great model for us in youth ministry. One of the reasons that we get uptight about working with students is that we feel we won't have the right answer or we won't say the right phrase. But incarnational ministry is being among the kids, spending time with them, and living our lives in such a way that we become a consistent signpost pointing to Jesus through our words and our actions. Quite often, the key to incarnational ministry is not saying the right thing, but simply being in the right place at the right time.

One of my most memorable "Emmaus discussions" with a group of students took place around a campfire one night along the Appalachian Trail after a delicious dinner of Spam, rice, and cream of mushroom soup (our hearts were "burning within us" too!). It seemed like the least likely place for heavy-duty spiritual conversation, but somehow we began talking with each other about what it meant to be a Christian, and it was amazing. I heard questions and shared in discussions that night that I hadn't experienced in a year of Sunday School and youth meetings.

Why then? Why that night? We didn't have enough light to read a Bible. Most of the kids had carefully packed their Bibles in the very bottom of their packs. We didn't even have an overhead projector! There's no good reason—except for the fact that my group decided at that particular time and place that it was time to talk. And that's why the most effective ministry is an incarnational ministry, a ministry that takes place "on the road."

6. Resist the temptation to be the "Answer Man." Even the most cursory study of Jesus' teaching in the Gospels will show that He taught more often by asking questions than by giving answers. It's interesting that on the road to Emmaus that day, Jesus never identified Himself to the two disciples during the entire trip. It's true that He "explained to them what was said in all the Scriptures concerning Himself" (Luke 24:27), but that was not till after they had thoroughly aired their own questions and doubts.

Our tendency as youth workers is to want to immediately correct wrong statements about God, to make sure that we point out areas of sin and error in a student's life. Unfortunately, that's a very quick way to close down communication. The average teenager is not that interested in playing "Ask Mr. Spiritual." That doesn't mean that we must be silent about our faith or about our feelings. It does mean that we may need to walk a while with the kids, and hear their questions before we start "explaining" everything.

One of the oldest principles of incarnational ministry is that we must "earn the right to be heard." As one preacher put it: "No one cares how much you know until they know how much you care."

Sometimes the most powerful testimony comes from a mouth that stays shut long enough to let the ears hear the questions and cries of a teenager who may not have all the right answers, but is at least asking some of the right questions.

7. Learn to love the sinner, even while hating the sin. Dick was a Young Life leader in the southeast who had a knack for getting close to students. As we led club together, I was continually amazed at his ability to befriend the kid that everybody else deemed undesirable and unreachable.

It took me about a year before I realized why I didn't seem to be enjoying the same success: It was as if I expected these guys to act like Christians or I wasn't going to share Christ with them. I wanted students to come to our group, but I wanted them to come on my terms. I was so busy letting these kids know verbally and nonverbally that I didn't approve of their lifestyle that their natural assumption would have been that neither I nor my God could accept someone as sinful as them. I had to learn how to love these guys without feeling that I was somehow condoning their behavior.

One of the most common barriers to our incarnational ministry among students is that we cannot get beyond their music, their appearance, and their language to see hurting and lonely people who need to be shown the love of Jesus. We can't embrace someone unless we're willing to touch him. And that means taking the first step of unconditional love and outreach.

When Jesus approached the Samaritan woman for a drink of water that hot afternoon (John 4:1ff), she was disarmed and surprised. "How can you ask me for a drink?" the woman asked, "(for Jews do not associate with Samaritans.)" If we are reaching out to the lepers and outcasts of the high school, we will probably be met with the same skepticism and suspicion. And yet, if we are willing to be flexible enough to accept students as they are, we are likely to find an openness and thirst that runs much deeper than their unattractive behaviors.

CLOSE TO THE HEART

I've often found a perverse comfort from that obscure little episode in the Book of Acts where Luke gives us a glimpse into the youth ministry of the Apostle Paul. (Read it for yourself, and tell me that you don't feel a little encouraged that Paul could put them to sleep with the best of us!)

Seated in a window was a young man named Eutychus [typical kid in the back of the room], who was sinking into a deep sleep as Paul talked on and on. When he was sound asleep, he fell to the ground from the third story and was picked up dead. Paul went down, threw himself on the young man and put his arms around him. "Don't be alarmed," he said. "He's alive!" Then he went upstairs again and broke bread and ate. After talking until daylight, he left. The people took the young man home alive and were greatly comforted.

(Acts 20:9-12)

Every time I read that passage, I am challenged that Luke is giving us here a parable from real life. So often we are discouraged in our ministries by those kids who sleep through the sermon, make inappropriate body noises during the Bible study, and giggle during the prayer time. Our natural response is to take them "for dead."

This passage reminds us, though, that sometimes a warm hug is more powerful than a hot talk. Paul's preaching put Eutychus to sleep, but his embrace brought him back to life. That is a principle we must never lose sight of if we want to disciple teenagers. Sermons and Bible studies and talks are important parts of the nurture process. There's no question about that. But even the most effective preaching is still the Word become word. The triumph of the Gospel of Christ is that it is the Word become flesh.

A Clearly Defined Vision

Lorne Sanny, President of the Navigators, recounts that back during the Civil War there was a bit of confusion in the high command of the Union Army. It seems that President Lincoln could not dissuade his generals from launching an attack on Richmond, Virginia. Why the generals had this obsession for capturing Richmond is unclear (though it can be a tough town if you don't know anybody), but Lincoln's generals persisted. Finally, Lincoln challenged his strategists with this observation: The Confederate Army is not in Richmond! (Author's note: That may be why they wanted to attack Richmond!) Lincoln asked, "What good will it do to capture the city? You will only gain geography. Gentlemen, our purpose is to win a war" (from "Laborers: the Navigators' Mission," Navigators *Daily Walk* Devotional Guide).

One of our problems in youth ministry is that we are constantly fighting the wrong battles, winning the wrong objectives, and consequently losing the war. The mind-set of the church is too often geared toward gaining geography that will not ultimately help us to win the war. That's why it's so important for those of us in youth ministry to define a specific objective, a specific goal, a vision that guides our strategy.

A BIBLICAL VISION

The Scripture gives us a clear sense of what our destination, our objective, our vision ought to be. Let's take a quick look at three separate passages.

1. Matthew 28:19. Here Jesus' followers were commanded, *"Go* *and make disciples* of all nations, baptizing them in the name of the Father and of the Son and of the Holy Spirit, and teaching them to obey everything I have commanded you" (italics added). Over the years the church has called this command "the Great Commission." In reality, as one preacher noted, it should be called "the Great Omission"! Like much of the Church, we in youth ministry have forgotten that our number-one priority is not to build big youth groups or flashy youth programs. We are called to build people. Anything less than that is an attack on Richmond! It might gain us some geography, but it won't win the war.

2. Ephesians 4:11-14. In these verses we are given a clear mandate for the Church at large, a mandate that has very real implications for those of us in youth ministry. Basically, our call is to *"equip saints for the work of ministry,* for the building up of the body of Christ, until we all attain to the unity of the faith and of the knowledge of the Son of God" (Ephesians 4:12-13, RSV).

But this passage in Ephesians 4 is even more appropriate as we continue in verses 13 and 14. Here is a special challenge for those of us who work with "teenage saints" (which may sound like a contradiction to some people!) to lead these saints into "mature personhood, to the measure of the stature of the fullness of Christ; so that they may no longer be children, tossed to and fro and carried about with every wind of doctrine, by the cunning of men, by their craftiness in deceitful wiles" (Ephesians 4:13-14, RSV). What a perfect description of the task we face in guiding teenagers through adolescence, building them up in the faith so that they can see through the propaganda of the world and help them to grow into mature people who have senses of identity and conviction.

3. 2 Timothy 2:2. Here is instruction given by Paul to Timothy, his "young son in the faith" — instruction that when viewed from the perspective of youth ministry gives us yet another confirmation of the call to build people equipped for ministry. Paul writes, "The things you have heard me say in the presence of many witnesses entrust to reliable men who will also be qualified to teach others" (2 Timothy 2:2). A quick glance at this verse will show four different generations of spiritual reproduction:

- First generation: Paul
- Second generation: Timothy
- Third generation: Reliable men
- Fourth generation: Others

Few verses of Scripture hint at the profound impact one person can have by simply equipping a young person (Timothy, in this case) for the work of ministry.

Waylon Moore, in an excellent book, *Multiplying Disciples* (NavPress), depicts this principle of multiplication even more dramatically. Notice the diagram which appears on page 58.

Obviously, this kind of ministry takes time. It takes commitment. And it requires a vision that extends beyond the question of how many youth show up for this week's bowling party. But, in a nutshell, that is where the map tells us we need to be going. We need to be captured by that vision. Our volunteer coworkers need to be called to that vision. And our parents and kids need to know that this is why our youth ministry exists. (I can still remember one of my youth group kids saying that he heard me refer to 2 Timothy 2:2 so often that he was just going to start calling it "Tutti-Tutu"!) Other objectives may be easier to attack. Other destinations may be more popular, and the routes to reach them may be exciting and fun, but this, at the bottom line, is where we are called to move.

AH, YES, BUT WHAT IS A "DISCIPLE"?
Pure and simple: The goal of youth ministry is building disciples. But what does a teenage disciple look like? Are they people who have short hair? How do they act on dates? Or do they date at all?

We have a lot of different ideas about discipleship. Some would say that a teenage disciple of Christ is a young person with short hair and middle-class values who doesn't "smoke, drink, cuss, chew, or go out with girls who do." Others use the word "disciple" to describe everybody from a committed Springsteen fan to a follower of the Rajneesh! Jot down in the space below your general definition of a Christian disciple.

_____

_____

_____

"Disciple" was Christ's favorite word for those whose lives were linked with His. The Greek word, *mathétes,* is used 269 times in the Gospels and Acts. Essentially, it means "one who is taught," a

CHAIN OF MULTIPLICATION
*adapted from Waylon Moore's **Multiplying Disciples***

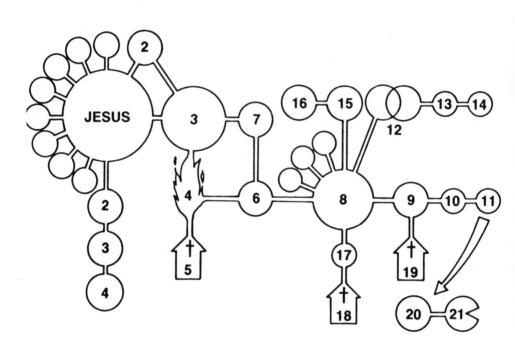

KEY

2. Andrew
3. Simon Peter
4. Pentecost
5. Antioch
6. Barnabas
7. John Mark
8. Paul

9. Timothy
10. Faithful men
11. Others also
12. Priscilla & Aquila
13. Apollos
14. Jews
15. Luke

16. Theophilus
17. Titus
18. Crete
19. Ephesus
20. Bald-headed youth minister
21. Today's teen

"trained one." There are two sets of passages listed below. The first set includes three verses in which Jesus gives a clear statement about how He characterizes discipleship. The second set of verses is a passage in which Jesus three times makes a statement about discipleship using the formula: "If _____, he *cannot* be My disciple." Read through these passages to sharpen your own sense of what it means to be a disciple, and write additions to your definition.

Set #1: John 8:31: _____

_____

_____

John 13:34-35: _____

_____

_____

John 15:1-8: _____

_____

_____

Set #2: Luke 14:25-33: _____

_____

_____

_____

Drawing from Scripture, there seem to be at least three essential characteristics of someone who is a disciple of Jesus Christ:
1. the person is growing in conformity to Christ;
2. the person is fruitful in efforts to bring others to Christ;

3. the person is working to conserve that fruit by doing adequate follow-up, the result of which will be another Christlike, fruitful disciple who is able to reproduce himself/herself.

To really make that vision a reality, a destination we can intentionally aim for, we need to be prepared to translate these characteristics of discipleship into the teenage life experience.

For example, we need to think through with our youth how a teenager lives differently on a day-to-day basis if that teenager is a disciple, a follower of Jesus Christ. It is not enough to give vague guidelines here. Until we have thought through this question in a very practical sense, we will not know what kinds of habits, traits, and disciplines to build into students. The target must be marked clearly enough so that one can know if one has "hit" or "missed," but loosely enough so that our description of "a disciple" is not legalistic or culturally bound.

Far too many youth ministers leave the notion of following Jesus and being His disciple on such spiritual terms that teens are either unwilling to volunteer because they don't understand what is expected of them, or they volunteer too easily because they don't understand the stakes. We must be practical here. How helpful is it to tell a teenager that he "cannot be a disciple" unless he is willing to "hate his father and mother, his wife and children, his brothers and sisters — yes, even his own life"? (Luke 14:25-33) That might sound too good to be true to some teenagers I know! We need to help kids translate these characteristics into everyday experience. That means that our focus is going to have to be less on building programs, and more on building people.

TURNING A VISION INTO A PROGRAM

No one has ever accused me of being an art critic, but I was intrigued by an article I came across in the *Philadelphia Inquirer* (October 7, 1984) about an eccentric artist who was scheduled to exhibit at the Philadelphia Museum of Art. In the early days, before Jonathan Borofsky launched his career as a "power artist," he spent day after day in his New York loft apartment doing nothing but counting. That's right. One-two-three-four, and so on. Borofsky explains that it was an act of near desperation, an attempt to try to bring some order into his life.

"Like a mantra . . . I'd bring all my thinking down to one thought," Borofsky explains, "reducing the noise in my head to one simple, clear, poetic, mathematical noise." As time went on, Borofsky became more ambitious in his counting, filling sheets of graph paper with numbers, one number to a square, 200 to 300 numbers to a page, with numbers on both sides of the paper, changing pen colors occasionally to add the artistic touch. (And you thought junior high kids were weird!)

As any youth worker surely knows, all creative people face adversities and skepticism. The Borofsky counting project was no different. At one point, during an argument with his girlfriend, sheets with the first 20,000 numbers were destroyed — four months of work down the tubes! On another occasion, a stroke of creative genius led him to begin affixing minus signs to the numbers, a whim that took him all the way back to minus 12,000 before he regained his forward motion. The most interesting part of this portrait of Borofsky was one comment made by the artist himself. Reflecting on the moment that he had passed a million after two years of counting, he said, "I thought maybe something would happen in my mind, but nothing. I just kept counting."

What is most remarkable about that statement, other than Borofsky's own apparent surprise at this discovery, is that it is a perfect illustration of the kind of frustration and disappointment that comes about when the sole focus of one's ministry is numbers — higher attendance, bigger crowds, constant counting. The tragedy is that this is precisely where so many of us in youth ministry place our bets. Like David (2 Samuel 24:10), we number the troops, hoping for a sense that certainly God is blessing this enterprise, thinking, like Borofsky, that at some point something will happen, "but nothing." And even more tragic, like Borofsky, a lot of youth ministries "just keep going."

There is a certain attraction to the kind of program that draws big crowds and features week after week of fun, high-visibility events. Once the machinery is in place, these programs are usually easier to maintain. As Borofsky puts it, you reduce it all down to "one, simple, clear, poetic, mathematical noise." I hope I'm not a stick-in-the-mud, but I don't think that sort of approach makes very good art or very good ministry.

Pat Hurley (*Penetrating the Magic Bubble,* Victor, pp. 12-17) characterizes this approach to ministry as program-oriented. Its basic goal is to build a strong program. He contrasts that approach with one that is person-oriented. The differences between these two approaches are real and will make a difference in the nuts-and-bolts ways we program our ministries. Consider the following chart.

Program-Oriented Ministry	Person-Oriented Ministry
GOAL is a good program: high visibility, functions smoothly, easy to promote.	GOAL is building people into disciples, "saints equipped for work of ministry."
STARTS with ideas: youth or volunteer receives mailing or hears of "wild, new idea"; decides to try it with group and see what happens.	STARTS with needs of kids involved. All programming strategies and ideas filtered through the question: How will it help us get students from where they are to deeper commitment?
SUCCESS judged by attendance: the more kids in the program, the better; lots of counting!	SUCCESS judged by individuals who have been involved with the ministry: Where are they now? How solid is their commitment? Are they "equipped saints"?
PRODUCES large numbers initially (if it's done well) and involves lots of people. Well-liked by kids; tends to play to "wants" rather than needs. Impresses congregation.	PRODUCES long-term results. May start small and be less impressive in the short run. Usually builds in more "staying power."
PREDICTABLE: Once a "working" system is established that seems to please everybody, no need to make changes.	FLEXIBLE: A program based on needs will change as needs change; may even necessitate changing a popular program to better meet objectives.

BUILDING A PERSON-ORIENTED PROGRAM

If you've ever dealt with a travel agent, you know that there are two pieces of information essential for that agent to properly service your business. Number one: that agent needs to know where you're going. Number two: that agent needs to know where you're coming from. It sounds odd, but a good trip-planner works backward, starting with the destination, then pinpointing the point of departure, and then, as a last step, choosing the route.

That is the way to plan for person-oriented ministry. It's the program-oriented approach which begins by choosing an idea, or an activity, a route, and *then* choosing a destination — obviously, not a good way to plan if you have a set destination in mind.

This book has already tried to define a biblical destination for youth ministry. Our goal is to build disciples. But how does one go about defining that "point of departure"? Person-oriented ministry begins when we try to inventory the needs of the youth involved in the ministry. Who are the kids currently involved within the ministry's sphere of influence? Where are those kids right now — spiritually, emotionally, physically, and socially?

Sound youth ministry begins with a thorough assessment of the present group, a step often neglected at great expense in time and energy. It's amazing how many youth ministry ideas are planned and programmed for groups that don't exist! Group profiles can be collected by preparing surveys that the youth respond to, or through one-on-one conversations, or by taking an evening to allow group members to collectively evaluate themselves. The key here is to listen. Keep the proverbial ear to the ground. Probe. Watch. Talk with parents, volunteer leaders, and church officials. Above all, don't choose a route until you've determined your point of departure.

Larry Richards, in his classic work, *Youth Ministry: Its Renewal in the Local Church* (Zondervan), has identified three broad categories of involvement that can be helpful as criteria for evaluating a youth group: Bible, life, and body. The following diagram might be a tool you can use for evaluating your group.

Bible: We begin by recognizing that if we hope to lead our students into maturity through adolescence with its cacophony of lies, temptations, pressures, and uncertainties, we must help them understand the Word of Truth. We must acquaint our youth with the Bible, its doctrines, its instructions, its main themes. We need also to enable our kids to begin to discover these truths on their own so that

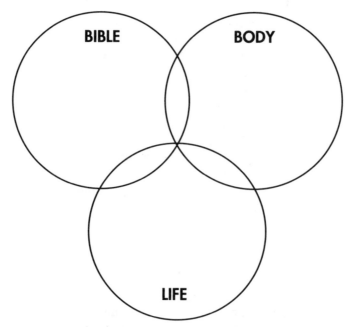

RICHARDS' DIAGRAM

as they confront the pressures of adulthood, they needn't hide behind old stories that "somebody told me," but can draw from a tough faith that can survive their world.

Life: Bible knowledge alone is not enough, though. God's truth is of little value to us if it isn't processed and worked out in the daily affairs of life. The second area of need that youth ministry must address is the task of building disciples who can take "Truth" into their marketplace, into their schools, on their dates, into their interpersonal relationships, into their evaluations of media messages through video, TV, movies, and music. We need to test our ministries to see if we are helping our teens evaluate their living habits in light of Scripture.

This is also the point at which we assess the "world-awareness" of our students. In what sense are they taking responsibility for bringing healing to their world at hand, as well as to the world at large? Responsible discipleship means taking seriously the mission implications of the Gospel. Christian teenagers may be strong on "Bible," know all the right verses, and speak fluent "Christianese." But they still need to be challenged that New Testament Christianity confronts them with the needs of hurting people around them.

Body: Even a consistent Christian lifestyle falls short of the biblical picture of discipleship, though. We haven't really gotten to our destination until we have confronted our students with the responsibilities they have as members of the body of Christ. Please, let's think of this as more than formal confirmation and membership! It is that, to be sure. But, it is also encouraging students into relationships with commitment—affirming each other, holding each other accountable, encouraging each other, stimulating one another to love and good works (Hebrews 10:24-25). In a teenage culture that celebrates using people for self-fulfillment and is more often characterized by comments that "cut" than by comments that heal, those kinds of relationships come through practical instruction and genuine opportunities for community.

Having a group evaluation of the three key areas can provide some healthy eye-opening, and it might be a good exercise for a volunteer team, a parent's youth ministry support group, a deacon board, or the youth themselves. There are lots of options for how this can be done. One possible format involves the survey which follows.

Note: Take some time as you discuss the survey to explain each area of involvement. It's a good opportunity to remind group members why the group exists!

SAMPLE SURVEY

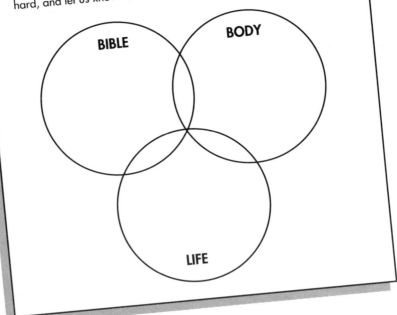

"ARE WE THERE YET?"

You remember that question! Anytime you're on a trip, that's the question you ask your dad every five minutes to help him relax! He kind of looks at the surroundings, checks out the map, swallows hard, and says, "No, I think we're going to have to head in this direction for a while."

Well, that's what this survey is about. We know we haven't arrived yet, but we do want to make sure we're moving in the right direction. So, we need your input about where we need to go next, what we might have passed too quickly, or where you think we got lost or sidetracked.

In each of the circles below, jot down your thoughts about your youth group using each of these categories for reference. Look at the surroundings, check out the map (the Bible) if you want to, swallow hard, and let us know what you think.

BIBLE

BODY

LIFE

Programming to Build Disciples

A Blueprint for Youth Ministry

everal years ago, the *Providence Journal* ran a story under the headline "Big Names to Have Dirty Linen Aired." The article detailed the results of a study done by the state of Massachusetts examining cases in which state funds may have been poorly used. Ironically, the study itself, a two-year project of a special commission, cost the state $1.5 million. The results were *almost* amusing (unless, of course, you're a Massachusetts taxpayer). By the time the report came out, there were a lot of red-faced public servants running for cover.

Among literally hundreds of case studies were these highlights (*Providence Journal,* "Massachusetts — Big Names to Have Dirty Linen Aired," Loring Swaim):

- *"The Boston State College 13-story tower, one of the largest buildings ever built by the Commonwealth.* Its top five floors, intended as a library, have been shut off since 1976 because the designer failed to include any centralized security checkpoints. Accordingly, the five floors have been heated, air-conditioned, and unused for four years. The college's auditorium is so constructed that one cannot see the stage from the balcony."

- *"The Haverhill (Mass.) parking deck.* It is so poorly designed it can only be demolished and rebuilt." Apparently, part of the problem here was in fitting some cars up the ramp of this magnificent structure!

- *"The multimillion dollar University of Massachusetts power plant.* It was built too far from the buildings it services — and never used."

The reason these state-financed gaffs are only *"almost* amusing" is that it is tragically reflective of what goes on consistently in youth ministries all across the country today! We continue to spend astronomical amounts of time, money, and energy on programs and structures so that we can say, "It's the largest ever built," but half the time the finished product cannot even be used. We are building power plants that don't deliver power—and that's not very funny!

Immediately following some very serious statements about discipleship, Jesus said, "For which one of you, when he wants to build a tower, does not first sit down and calculate the cost, to see if he has enough to complete it? Otherwise, when he has laid a foundation, and is not able to finish, all who observe it begin to ridicule him, saying, 'This man began to build and was not able to finish' " (Luke 14:28-30).

To build the kind of youth ministry program that will accomplish the purpose for which it was built, serious consideration needs to be given to the "blueprint."

MODELS OF MINISTRY

I've often wondered about the architect who designed that impotent power plant in Massachusetts. What do you say to a Board of University Trustees when you've just spent several million dollars on a power plant that doesn't deliver power? Do you walk into the meeting with a sheepish grin and say, "Do you guys want to hear something funny?" Or, do you take a more constructive approach: "What would you guys think about just having our 'night classes' during the day?"

There is no shortage of proposals about how youth programs should be designed. The youth ministry landscape is littered with youth programs that were built and cannot be used. That's why it's worth taking a critical look at some of the various models of youth ministry programming. Dr. Mark Senter, Professor of Christian Education at Trinity Divinity School has done a good job of identifying some of the standard designs (*Youth Education in the Church*, ed. Zuck and Benson, Chicago: Moody Press). Here are some of the more prominent models.

The Hero Model

This model of programming, especially prevalent among parachurch youth ministries, is sometimes referred to as the "bright-light" approach. Essentially, it's based on the theory that on a dark night, it is the brightest light in the neighborhood that will attract the most moths. If we really want to reach students, we should build our youth programs around a central personality, some charismatic figure who is going to be naturally attractive to teenagers. And, of course, as the "Bright-light Knight" attracts students, so will those students attract other students, and so on, like so many moths buzzing around a streetlamp.

A. Strengths:

1. The Hero Model is typically incarnational and relational. It's almost always focused on some individual who is willing and able to get close to kids, and to build significant relationships with them. That's good.

2. To some extent, this approach offers a genuine reflection of the way teenagers think. After all, it is a fact that students are more often attracted to a program not because of what it stands for, but for WHO it stands with. We have television shows like "Walter Cronkite's Universe" and "Bill Moyers' World of Ideas" because, sad to say, in today's culture, personality is far more important than ideas. If teenagers are attracted by strong personality, it makes sense to assume that David Letterman would make a better youth leader than Mr. Rogers.

B. Weaknesses:

1. On the other hand, this strategy of programming breeds mavericks, lone rangers—people who tend to shine better and brighter when they are working on their own. That means it will be very difficult to develop any kind of effective team ministry in the program. And without the diversity and cooperation of a team approach, a youth program will be severely handicapped in the type of students and number of students it can expect to draw.

2. It takes a certain stereotypical kind of personality to make this Hero Model work. All the ministry is based on one person, and, unless that one person is Jesus, that's kind of risky. For one thing, as leaders we all tend to reproduce not only our strengths, but also our own weaknesses. Without the balance of a team of people, it's easy for students to focus more on a human being and less on God.

3. There is the danger that when the hero/leader leaves the program, the program leaves with him or her. A program that is built on a personality can just as quickly fall when that personality is no longer around to prop it up.

4. The biggest problem is that we are not doing youth ministry to attract moths. If we were just trying to draw a big crowd we could book AC/DC to play at youth fellowship. Our bright lights might help us gain geography; it will not help us win the war.

The Involvement Model

Youth programs that utilize the Involvement Model always have lots of different ways for students to get involved in the program — everything from puppet ministry to youth council to clowning to drama teams to youth choir. The key word here is *involvement.* In some programs most of the involvement is aimed at ministry within the group (e.g., the "games team" handles recreation each week at youth group, the "audio-visual team" prepares special A-V presentations each meeting, etc.). In other programs, most of the student involvement is more oriented toward outreach.

A. Strengths:

1. The obvious strength of this approach is that it involves students in *doing* something. It makes youth fellowship more than just a spectator sport, particularly for those students whose gifts are not in the traditional areas of music and singing.

2. Utilizing all of these means of involvement can give a group a powerful ministry of outreach into the community. That can mean a positive evangelistic impact.

B. Weaknesses:

1. The weakness in the Involvement Model is that it doesn't give adequate attention to nurture and discipleship. The danger here is that we occasionally end up sending out half-filled Christians who are trying to overflow. Sometimes students who are very involved in youth group activities or youth group leadership positions make the mistake of thinking that this is the same as having a vital relationship with the living God. That's not only wrong, it's exploitative.

The Relevancy Model

My own youth group years were during the sixties. Everybody was trying hard during that era to be relevant. Otherwise well-adjusted adults were wearing beads and medallions, saying words like "groovy," and walking around in "bell bottoms" and Nehru jackets. It was not a pretty picture.

But we were relevant. We would walk into Sunday School and the teacher would ask, "What do you guys want to talk about this week?" And with that springboard we would plunge into yet another session of whining about world problems. In short, it was a youth ministry based on relevance and felt need. It's not as popular as it once was, but this appears to still be the preferred approach in many mainline churches.

A. Strengths:

1. It's, well . . . uh . . . relevant! And that's important. Probably one of the major complaints from teenagers about the church is that it's irrelevant. It doesn't touch them where they live or scratch them where they itch.

B. Weaknesses:

1. A youth ministry that is relevant can very easily become a youth ministry without focus, constantly changing goals to fit the changing tides.

2. The Relevancy Model often presupposes that the Bible is irrelevant and, therefore, that any time spent studying such a crusty, dusty old book is time poorly invested. Unfortunately, however, this appraisal runs in direct contradiction to Scripture: "The grass withers and the flowers fall, but the Word of our God stands forever" (Isaiah 40:8).

In short, it's been almost three decades since the sixties. Nobody wears Nehru jackets anymore and the Beatles broke up, but the Bible still stands as the Word of God. That ought to tell us something!

PYRAMID POWER

I have talked with a significant number of youth ministers over the last several years who use as the blueprint for their programs a pyramid-type concept. (While I would like to believe that the pyramid shape authenticates the biblical, Mideastern roots of this model, it's not really clear who was the first to develop the idea.) It has several variations, but the diagram on the next page gives the basic picture.

Essentially, what this diagram does for us is help us evaluate and develop our youth ministry programs by showing us the kinds of students our programs are addressed to. Looking at the diagram, we need to think of each of the levels of the pyramid as representing students at varying levels of Christian commitment. The higher the level on the pyramid, the higher the level of commitment. Let's look briefly at each level of the pyramid.

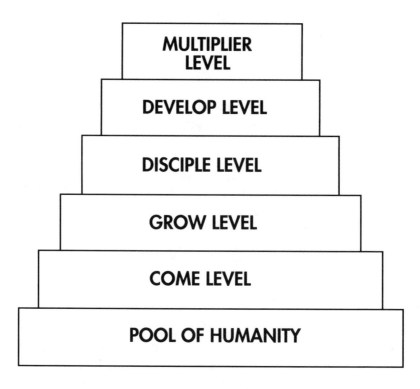

Pool of Humanity

This level of the pyramid represents the teenage population in general, the teenagers within your geographical sphere of influence. Your group, in fact, may not have any influence on these students at the present time. The vast majority of these kids may not even know you or your ministry exist. But you know about them, and by God's grace and power you want to reach them with the Gospel.

For example, my current Pool of Humanity while here at Eastern College in St. Davids, Pennsylvania includes at least three to four public high schools within a five-mile radius. Because of the socio-economic makeup of St. Davids and the surrounding suburbs of western Philadelphia (known as the Main Line), there are also probably twice that many private prep schools.

Now, for someone to do person-oriented youth ministry in this area, these are simply some facts that must be reckoned with. This information, and other social and religious data about these youth, would help someone design a program uniquely suited to this area. And that's important because you don't have to be in youth ministry very long to discover that what works great in Tacoma or Tallahassee may bomb in Philadelphia (and vice versa). So, for a program to begin right, it is wise to begin by assessing your unique pool of humanity.

Come Level

Billy is one of those kids who never shows up for prayer breakfast or Sunday School, and always seems to have unavoidable conflicts that prevent his helping out with fund-raisers and work projects. Spiritually, he ranks somewhere between "plant life" and "lower primate," and whenever you "pass the hat" with Billy in the crowd, you're always just a little relieved to get your hat back!

The picture isn't completely negative, though. There are two areas for which Bill has shown tremendous interest and zeal: one is food, and the other is girls. Whenever a youth group activity allows for a large selection of either, you can count on Billy to be there! Billy doesn't make any pretense about it. He does not have any real commitment to Christ, but he does have a strong commitment to having a good time.

There are kids like Billy in any youth ministry I've ever been around. Theirs is a *Come Level* commitment. Their only commitment to the group is to come when the group is doing something they like — something fun or entertaining.

It's not uncommon to hear youth workers complain about kids like Billy. After all, we're called to build disciples and we "can't afford to waste time with some student who isn't willing to get serious about his walk with Christ." But that complaint raises some important questions. To be sure, our goal is to build students into multipliers, and that takes a certain degree of spiritual drive.

But let's be honest and shrewd enough to admit that (a) most teenagers on the outside of our ministries just are not mysteriously born with that degree of spiritual vitality; and (b) a majority of the students on the inside of our groups aren't there either. If we only program for the spiritual heavyweights, we are going to touch the lives of very few kids.

And even more important, (c) we need to remember that today's multiplier was yesterday's (or yesteryear's) "disinterested" *Come Level* kid. By the same token, today's *Come Level* teens might become tomorrow's disciples if we can somehow bring them within the influence of our ministry so that we can give them love, training, and attention.

Grow Level

Students at the *Grow Level* are students within our program environment who are willing to submit themselves to spiritual growth. These are the teens who take part in a youth activity, even if it involves them in some amount of Bible study or spiritual input. Essentially, that is the difference between kids at the *Come Level* and kids at the *Grow Level.*

Sally, a young woman with a *Grow Level* commitment, was not excited about the four Bible studies scheduled for the Winter Retreat Weekend, but she was willing to go along anyway. Her boyfriend, Sonny, who had a love for downhill skiing and an acute allergy to spiritual matters, decided not to sign up for the retreat. He reasoned that four Bible studies was too high a price to pay even if it meant being close to his favorite sport and his favorite girlfriend. His is a good example of *Come Level* commitment.

I am grateful for both students — for the chance to have some input into their lives. I am pleased that Sally is at least open enough to "take a chance" on the retreat. But I also respect Sonny's fear of being uncomfortable with the spiritual activity that will be a part of the retreat. I can affirm both teens for where they are, while praying and working to take them both to deeper levels of commitment.

This is a good point to be reminded of two important realities.

1. Willingness to grow is not the same thing as commitment to growth. Kids at the *Grow Level* are not seeking spiritual growth on their own initiative. They will come to Bible study on Wednesday night, or take part in Sunday night meetings, but only because it requires little more than their passive involvement. We should not assume that a teenager at weekly Bible study is hungry for spiritual food and willing to take the initiative to get it.

That's a consideration to remember in preparing weekly Bible studies for youth group. That is not to say that we should short-change Bible study time in favor of "fun and games." It is to say that we need to see part of our agenda as being evangelistic and that we should not assume students are walking into Bible study saying, "Fill my cup." Attention needs to be given to providing Bible study opportunities that incite student interest, invoke active participation, and equip students with the tools for taking responsibility for their own spiritual growth.

2. Consistent attendance is not an indication of consistent commitment. I didn't understand the *Grow Level* commitment early on in my ministry with students. I misinterpreted a student's strong commitment to me or to the program as being a strong commitment to Christ.

That was a delusion clearly exposed for me when one of my most active students graduated from high school, went away to college, and almost immediately made an apparent, conscious decision to abandon any principles of Christian living. Obviously, it was a real disappointment to me, but it was also a real education.

It may be naiveté or just wishful thinking, but it's a common mistake of youth ministers to assume that just because kids are involved in spiritual activity, they are personally involved in spiritual growth. It's wonderful that kids are willing to submit themselves to spiritual growth, but let's not mistakenly assume that this means they will automatically, of their own initiative, develop a pattern of continued growth and fellowship following graduation.

Disciple Level

When a student in the youth group begins to take the initiative for his or her own spiritual growth, this student has matured to what might be described as a *Disciple Level* commitment. We've already examined the kinds of characteristics that one might expect to find in a teenager at this level of commitment (chapter 4). Suffice it to say that the key here is the word "discipline." A student at the *Disciple Level* is a student who is willing to discipline himself—to do personal Bible study on his own, memorize Scripture (even if it isn't a requirement for the choir tour), or personally seek to be a witness at school, at home, or wherever.

The role of the youth worker at this stage is to provide instruction and tools for students to pursue their own spiritual development. A teen may exhibit genuine willingness to study the Bible for himself, but that desire can burn out if the teen isn't given some personal help and guidance about how that kind of development happens.

Develop Level

As students begin to advance in spiritual growth, they will in time move into the next level of commitment. Teens at the *Develop Level* are students willing to take the initiative, not only for their own spiritual growth, but for the spiritual growth of others as well.

It's very important to mention here that the Develop Level of any lasting youth ministry will include both youth *and adults*. These youth and adults are people with whom the youth worker can begin to do a focused work of training and equipping for ministry. Without going into much detail about this training process, it might be helpful to simply remember two basic concepts:

1. Training is a progressive work that begins with the instructor *modeling* the task, and eventually turning over responsibility for the task to the trainee.

2 Ministry training should begin with physical responsibilities (e.g., arrange the chairs, line up transportation, plan a skit, set up the movie), and then expand to include spiritual responsibilities (lead the Bible study, share a devotion, give a testimony).

Very important to note here is that the *Develop Level* comes *after* the *Disciple Level* and not the reverse. I have seen the pyramid concept published in which these two levels were given in the reverse order. In my estimation, that's a serious mistake.

We already have far too many youth and adults in church leadership who, perhaps unwittingly, have assumed responsibility for the spiritual growth of others, but have not demonstrated any willingness to take responsibility for their own spiritual growth. That is not the pattern we are given in 1 Timothy 3 and other passages where Paul writes about spiritual leadership.

This is a particularly easy trap to fall into in youth ministry because we are occasionally confronted with students and would-be volunteers who have all kinds of leadership ability, but all the spiritual depth of a Cabbage Patch doll. This is especially common with an elected youth council or youth advisory board, since their makeup is usually determined more by popularity and status than by spiritual maturity. It is tempting to pass over the less charismatic student who shows genuine spiritual depth in favor of the one who is head cheerleader or star quarterback, but if we are talking about development of spiritual leadership, we had better remember that "God sees not as man sees."

Multiplier Level

The final level of commitment is that point at which students begin to catch a vision for going back into their own junior high and high schools and starting the process over, reproducing it in the lives of their own friends or classmates. When we help move kids into this level of commitment, we are multiplying our own efforts in much the same way that Paul multiplied his by pouring himself into Timothy.

To be very realistic, it has been quite easy to move through these levels of commitment in only a few book pages. Unfortunately, the movement doesn't usually come that easily in real life ministry with kids. (How's that for understatement?)

One of my favorite illustrations of this process of growth draws from the world of the emperor penguin. While the parallels may not seem obvious at first, they are very real.

When the female emperor penguin has laid the eggs, she leaves the nest to fatten herself on fish from the frigid arctic waters. The remarkable fact is that at this point, the male emperor penguin steps in and gingerly places the newly laid egg on top of his feet, where he stands without moving, carefully balancing it there for the next two months until it hatches!

Ah, yes! If that is not a picture of youth ministry, I don't know what is. Here you have this new life, with only the promise, the potential for maturity. It cannot care for itself or survive without patient oversight. But, if we hang tough, stand strong, trust God, and wait, there will emerge yet another being who is capable of that same reproductive process.

BRINGING IT ALL TOGETHER

After you've been in youth ministry for a while, you begin to grow intensely skeptical of models and blueprints. I suppose it's like shopping for a car: the design may be beautiful in the drawing room, the lines may be sleek and attractive in the showroom, but the ultimate question is, "How does it run?"

The best way to understand the pyramid illustration, with its various levels of commitment, is to imagine the pyramid being turned upside down and taking on the shape of a funnel. (Turn this book upside down and try it. Surprise!) For the less mechanically inclined, study the diagram on page 80. When you begin to visualize your ministry this way, you can do some careful evaluation of your youth program.

For a youth program to be well-rounded, accomplishing the purpose for which it was designed, there must be some type of formal or informal programming that will meet the needs of kids at each of

POOL OF HUMANITY

COME LEVEL

GROW LEVEL

DISCIPLE LEVEL

DEVELOP LEVEL

MULTIPLIER LEVEL

EPHESIANS 4:11-13

these levels of commitment. There need to be *Come Level* programs, geared to the student who is "not into religion at all," and there need to be programs that will motivate the forward progress and growth of those at the *Grow, Disciple,* and *Develop Levels.*

The beauty of this kind of evaluation is that it helps you see where a particular youth program is overweight and where it's underweight, what kinds of students have been programmed for and, perhaps, what levels of commitment have been inadvertently ignored. This is where you make the hard decisions that will determine whether your current program fits the kind of blueprint that will yield the program and product you intend.

SOME IMPORTANT CONSIDERATIONS

When one sees the pyramid/funnel concept clearly, it becomes obvious that there are two important implications for youth ministry.

1. The Law of Spiritual Commitment

We've seen it in our ministries for a long time, but we see it clearly here: As commitment increases, attendance decreases. This was true of Jesus' ministry and it will be true of ours. Five thousand people came out to get fed by Jesus (Matthew 14:14-21) but how many of those 5,000 followed Jesus into Jerusalem and Golgotha when opposition grew stronger and risks became greater?

I am amazed when youth workers question me with genuine sincerity saying, "I don't understand it. We get 40 kids out to our swim party at the lake, but we only got 14 at our Bible study Tuesday night." I want to smile and say, "Hey, welcome to the world! Kids like swimming better than they like studying the Bible!" Let's face that, understand it, and then move on.

What we do clearly need to understand is that when we judge a program by attendance, we may be using a very deceptive criterion. A *Disciple Level* program that is really helping you build stronger believers may not draw the crowds that a high visibility *Come Level* program draws, but, in reality, it may be a much more vital part of the youth ministry environment.

This is an important dynamic not only for youth workers to understand, but also for parents, pastors, and youth committees. At first glance, it may not seem wise to put more money and time into a small group of people when, in terms of attendance, much greater payoff is seen elsewhere. But we need to see that these students and programs at the *Disciple* and *Multiplier Levels* are the "bread and butter" of our ministry. That doesn't mean that we shortchange the *Come Level* program. It does mean that so much of the time when we are putting a huge amount of energy into programs that bring in lots of kids, programs with high visibility and much excitement, we might be "capturing Richmond," but that alone won't help us win the war.

2. The Importance of the "Unspiritual"

In one congregation where I used to work as youth minister, there was one mother who always got on my case whenever we did an "unspiritual" activity like white-water rafting or playing Ultimate Frisbee. She considered it a total waste of time — certainly not what I was getting paid to do!

If this mother had understood the principle of the funnel, she could have understood, perhaps, that in the right program environment, even the "unspiritual" activities have very legitimate, spiritual goals. After all, the most spiritually intensive program in the world doesn't do anybody any good if students won't take part in it. It may make some parishioners feel good to know that "the youth are having their all-night prayer meeting instead of going to the Amy Grant concert." But if there aren't any kids at the all-night prayer meeting, that *really is* a waste of time!

As a balance for the Law of Spiritual Commitment, we need to realize that we can't get students to be multipliers if we can't involve them in leadership development. And we can't get them involved at the *Develop Level* if we don't get them discipled. And we can't get them discipled if we can't get them interested in growth. And we can't get them to grow if we can't get them to come. And that might mean that the most spiritually strategic action I can take with some students is to take them away with me for a day of white-water rafting, building relationships, and breaking down defenses.

With these thoughts in mind, we're ready to move into the process of evaluation.

EVALUATING A YOUTH PROGRAM: THREE STAGES

Stage One: Where Are the Kids?

The first stage in evaluating your current youth ministry is to get some idea of the kinds of students involved in your program. Either by yourself, or with the help of your adult volunteers, simply work through the roster of the group and, as closely as possible, try to place each individual at one of the five levels of commitment in the pyramid. Use the blank pyramid on page 84. If it's helpful, use symbols by each name to indicate a "growth spurt," a renewed commitment, or even a current "mellowing" of spiritual fervor. For large groups, you may want to draw up a pyramid for each grade grouping.

EXAMPLE: High School Group–First Church

Shannon S.

MULTIPLIERS

Tony C.
Heather H.

DEVELOP LEVEL

Kristen W. ↔
Craig M.
Mary Noel R. ↑

DISCIPLE LEVEL

Erin A. ↑   Sylvia P.
Ashley R.   Ronald R. ↑
Keith K.   Richard N.
Trish S.   Jimmy C. ↓

GROW LEVEL

Joe A.   Joy A.
Bill M.   Stephanie
Sally P.   Pedro G.
Sandra G.   Brian B.
Steve E.   Maggie R.
Cindy B.

COME LEVEL

Bob J.   Steve R. Sally G. George M. Bruce B.

POOL OF HUMANITY

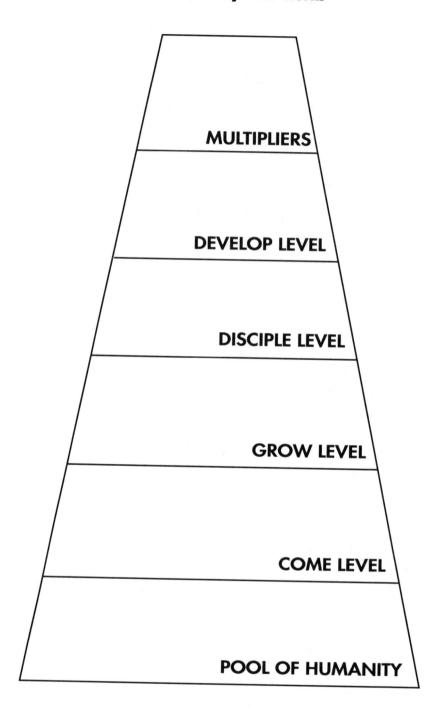

Stage Two: Where Is the Program?

For the second phase of evaluation, the funnel diagram is more helpful. Using the blank funnel below, do an inventory of your youth program. What kinds of programs do you have that would minister to students at the various levels of commitment? Are there any programs that seem to overlap more than one level of commitment? Are most of the programs geared to *Come* and *Grow Level* commitment? Where in the program do you feed and nurture kids at the deeper levels of commitment?

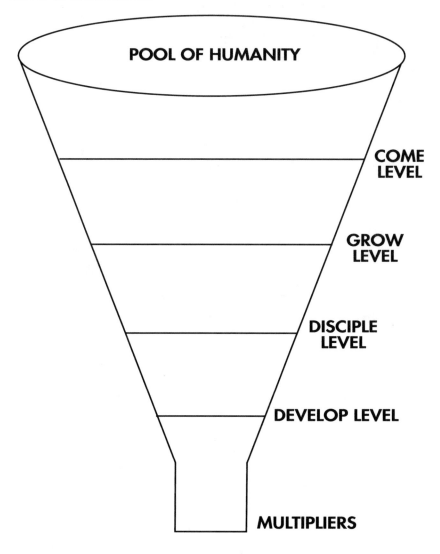

POOL OF HUMANITY

COME LEVEL

GROW LEVEL

DISCIPLE LEVEL

DEVELOP LEVEL

MULTIPLIERS

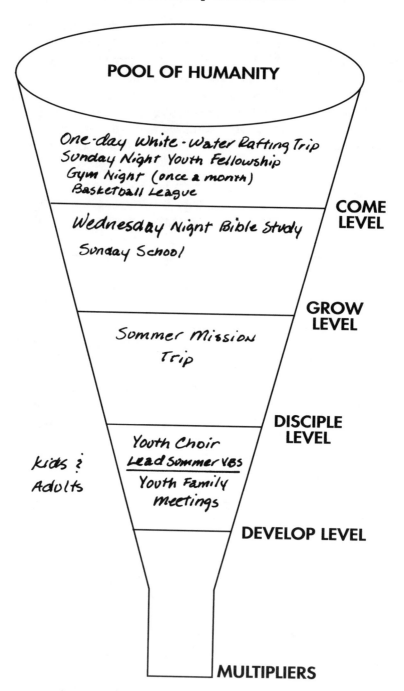

POOL OF HUMANITY

One-day White-Water Rafting Trip
Sunday Night Youth Fellowship
Gym Night (once a month)
Basketball League

COME LEVEL

Wednesday Night Bible Study

Sunday School

GROW LEVEL

Summer Mission Trip

DISCIPLE LEVEL

kids &
Adults

Youth Choir
Lead Summer VBS
Youth Family
meetings

DEVELOP LEVEL

MULTIPLIERS

Stage Three: Does It Run?

With stage two complete, you are ready to do the serious work of deciding if this program you've built actually accomplishes the purpose for which it was designed. If we're honest, we may find along with that special Massachusetts commission that some of our "towers" can't be used and some of our "power plants" aren't delivering power.

Looking at the high school ministry for First Church, it's readily apparent that it is top-heavy. As is fairly typical with youth programs, the program at First Church is strongest at the shallowest levels of commitment. The ministry for First Church students at deeper levels of commitment is thin, centered mostly on two relatively short-term summer activities. (The Youth Choir can broaden the opportunities slightly, but only for students willing to participate in a choir-type activity.) Beyond these general observations, these are the kinds of specific questions one might consider:

• **Is the Sunday night youth fellowship really a *Come Level* event?** For that Sunday night fellowship to genuinely attract *Come Level* youth, it probably needs a pretty thorough overhaul, beginning with the name. Since when is an activity called "Youth Fellowship" a big draw to non-Christian, non-churched kids?

We do ourselves a disservice when we call *Come Level* events "United Methodist Youth Fellowship" or "Baptist Youth Fellowship." If we truly want to reach non-Methodist, or non-Baptist, or non-Christian students, that goal should be reflected in our name. A non-Christian teen would logically assume that a program called "Freaks for Jesus" is one in which he may not feel comfortable. That is why most youth workers I know do not attend conventions of the American Society of Civil Engineers. They assume that they don't belong there!

If an event is *Come Level*, it should be *Come Level* right down to the name. That's why Young Life is called Young Life. If you are young and alive, you're in! A name like "Sunday Night Live" or "Breakaway" would be much more appropriate if First Church really wants to make its Sunday night meeting a *Come Level* event.

Obviously, the nature of the event itself is even more important than the name. So often, youth workers have what they consider *Come Level* events, but the actual content and mood of the events is *Grow* or *Disciple Level*. For example, while visiting with one church youth group, I was interested to hear the youth leader repeatedly encourage his youth to invite their non-Christian friends to this weekly meeting. That led me to believe that this meeting would be *Come Level* in content.

I was surprised when the group began singing because their choice of songs was anything but *Come Level*. They sang "Father, I Adore You," "He Is Lord," "Alleluia," and some other really beautiful songs of praise. But songs of praise are more appropriate when Christians sing together. It doesn't seem fair to expect a non-Christian to come to a meeting to which he has been invited, and then force that student to sing praises to a God he is not even willing to recognize.

The real clincher came during about the third chorus when the youth leader looked up from his guitar, stopped the singing, stared straight at some of the guys in the back of the group and said, "You guys might be new here, but you need to get up off your rear and start singing or you can leave." This youth leader unconsciously had betrayed these youth and those who had invited them.

Come Level kids, when they attend an activity, are not promising they will worship, sing, pray, or study the Bible. They are promising to be there as long as we have what they like. We need to welcome them on those terms. If they are not "fitting in" with what the group is doing, that may be the group's fault, not the students'. That's what it means to make a *Come Level* activity truly an activity for *Come Level* kids.

• **Does the basketball program really attract *Come Level* kids?** This is an easy question to answer, but also a very important one. If the basketball league is legitimately a *Come Level* program, it should be attracting new kids from First Church's *Pool of Humanity*. With the time, money, and energy it takes to actually run a good basketball program even in a small league, one needs to be sure one is getting what one has paid for.

If one discovers that the basketball program involves almost totally students already involved in other areas of the program, it might be wise to redesign the basketball program to fit the level of commitment of the kids involved. Realize that it isn't really a *Come Level* outreach, and remake it—perhaps into a *Grow Level* program. For example, it might be a requirement that any of the guys on the basketball team must also work through a workbook on Christian growth to maintain eligibility. Or requirements can include Scripture memory, a service project, or consistent attendance at the weekly Bible study.

• **Are *Grow Level* youth really the ones in Sunday School?**
This may be the question that most needs to be asked of the average
youth program. That's because Sunday School often is a classic case
of providing a program that does not fit those in attendance. Common
sense and experience tells us that, in most cases, Sunday School is
probably the time during the week when our program draws the
most genuinely *Come Level* students. Parents will force their kids to
participate in Sunday School when they will not force them to be
involved in any other area of the program. But, ironically, the average
Sunday School consists largely of *Grow Level* (or deeper) study
materials.

I'm convinced that one of the major reasons for so many of the
discipline problems that confront Sunday School teachers is that they
are trying to use *Grow Level* materials with *Come Level* students.
That won't work! A person-oriented approach to Sunday School
would be to admit that most of our participants are *Come Level* kids
who are there begrudgingly, daring us to "bless" them. If that's the
case, then change the format and content of Sunday School to more
of a *Come Level* atmosphere. It may sound radical, but it certainly
sounds reasonable.

This is the kind of thinking that we should be doing in stage three
of the evaluation process to really find out if the program "runs."
There are other questions that might be asked of the program at
First Church, but let's shift our attention for the last chapter to some
strategies that First Church could possibly use for programming at
the *Disciple Level* and beyond.

ESSENTIAL 6

Programs That Work

The title of this section could be misleading, because programs don't make disciples. Only disciples make disciples. But the most capable disciple-maker in the world will be ineffective without some sort of plan or program for allowing this process to happen. This chapter is about three specific programs aimed at youth who are at commitment levels of *Grow Level* and higher.

Outlining specific programs can be dangerous. David tried to fight in Saul's armor (1 Samuel 17:38-39), and "could not, for he was not used to them." Sometimes, when we try to take someone else's program and use it in our ministry, it just doesn't work because we are trying to fight in someone else's armor. Some fight with armor, and some fight with a sling, but above all, everyone must use strategies that are comfortable for them.

At the same time, doing program evaluation and rethinking our ministry objectives won't be very helpful if we aren't able to implement some changes. On the following pages are descriptions and examples of three programs used by a particular church in a particular *Pool of Humanity*. While these models may need to be adapted so that the "armor" will fit your style and ministry, this will provide some practical models for actually developing programs that build disciples.

The first two programs, *Small Group* and *Covenant Group*, are built around a fellowship group format. The third, *Onward Bound*, is a personally tailored program for spiritual growth. Each attempts to be person-oriented as it implements the vision of disciple-making.

SMALL GROUPS:
A PROGRAM THAT WORKED

Dr. Merton Strommen, in his classic work *Five Cries of Youth,* writes that the loudest of all the "five cries of youth" is the cry of self-hatred—young people trying to live with a self that they don't respect, don't admire, and can't exchange. Most interesting, though, is Strommen's insight about how we in youth ministry can respond to this attitude in our ministries with teens. "The techniques of hearty encouragement, bushels of compliments, and a series of social gatherings are not enough. Low self-esteem youth need a community or small group where they can live in the awareness of being accepted" (*Five Cries of Youth,* Strommen, Harper, p. 30).

For that reason, it's difficult to conceive of an effective youth program that does not make use of some kind of small group strategy. Obviously, if the youth group is small to begin with, it may not be necessary to design an actual program to fulfill this role. But if there are more than 10 youth involved, this might be a strategic way to move.

For the most part, any sort of serious small group program is going to be a *Grow Level* (or above) activity. That is the case simply because for any small group ministry to be effective, the participants must have some degree of willingness to maintain consistent attendance. Without the component of consistent attendance, the most creative small group in the world is doomed to failure.

Before we look at these specific small group-type strategies that can be used with *Grow* and *Disciple Level* students, let's think through some of the basic components of effective small groups. Purely and simply, small groups are about fellowship, what the New Testament characterizes as *koinonia.* While the church, in general, has horribly misused this term, nowhere has it been more misused than in youth ministry. We have Sunday night "fellowship." We "fellowship" around the bowling alley. And sometimes we have "fellowship" during the 20 minutes between Sunday School and worship.

Howard Snyder has diagnosed the problem very clearly: "The church today is suffering a fellowship crisis. . . . It is simply not experiencing nor demonstrating that 'fellowship of the Holy Spirit' (2 Corinthians 13:14) that marked the New Testament church. . . . The church is highly organized just at the time when her members are caring less about organization and more about community" (*The Problem with Wineskins,* Snyder, IVP, p. 89).

If this is true for the church in general, it is especially true for youth ministry. Donald Posterski, a leader in Canadian youth ministry, reports that his research for Project Teen Canada indicates there is no value that teenagers rank more highly than their small cluster of close friends. Posterski goes on to point out that his research shows that, while kids certainly enjoy the big, rowdy group meetings where there is a large group of teenagers, over the long haul their preference is for small, informal groups. (As Posterski remarks, this represents a change from 10 years ago when youth ministry capitalized more on a "herd mentality" that focused on a group of "in" kids who by their attendance might attract other kids who want to be associated with the popular crowd.)

Not only do small groups help us to minister to the area of "felt need" that Posterski points to, they help us to give unique focus to one of the three components of a discipleship lifestyle that we discussed earlier in this book. Most youth groups have some arena in which kids are being "taught" the Bible and, in most cases, there is every effort to apply that biblical teaching to daily life. But small groups give us the perfect setting to learn and develop body life.

What a Small Group Is Not

Whenever we talked about small groups in our youth program, we always took pains to make sure that the students knew what we were about. We were careful to stress that this was not another Bible study. We tried, rather, to make our small groups "people studies" based on the Bible. We really felt that our students were getting enough Bible study. Small Group was where we focused on "Body study." That is an important balance to be maintained.

We wanted to emphasize that small groups in our program were not there strictly for socializing. This was not some kind of Christian fraternity within the youth group. While the intention was to leave the groups unstructured enough to promote open spontaneous sharing, we reminded leaders of the old law: "One of the best ways to guarantee spontaneity is to plan very carefully." Our small group ministries were designed specifically to open students to one another.

Finally, we needed to make it clear that small group ministry is not some kind of mystical "navel gazing" where people sit around in a circle and do cute things like shaping their bubble gum into their image of love. Too much of what the church has tried to do under the

93

guise of "fellowship" has not been biblical sharing in which brothers and sisters come together under the lordship of Christ. Ultimately, the purpose of our small group ministries was to bring students closer to the members of the body of Christ so that they could grow closer to the Christ of the body.

What a Small Group Is

As general guidelines for structuring an effective small group ministry, consider these five components (from *Sixty-Nine Ways to Start a Small Group and Keep It Growing,* Larry Richards, Zondervan):

1. Identification. A sound small group program will build in ways for teens to identify themselves. This is as much for their own benefit as it is for the others in the small group. Every person needs to understand the difference between history (facts about birthday, parent's occupation, grade in school, etc.) and "his story" ("who I am," "where I'm going," and "why I'm me").

2. Affirmation. We need to help kids come up with ways of making affirming statements about their brothers and sisters in Christ without feeling strange. Typically, the guys are afraid to compliment a girl because they are afraid the girls will think they're in love. And, of course, the girls have that same fear of being overly admiring. We have to give them ways and means of affirming who they are once they've identified themselves. This concept that "these people know the real me, and like me" is a tremendous point of awakening for most teenagers.

3. Exploration. This component of small groups deals with the continuing need to give students avenues by which they can explore themselves, their feelings, and their values, while learning about the others in the group.

4. Concentration. This is that dimension of a small group that keeps it focused. The concentration of the small group should be Scripture, and how that Scripture can be used to help them probe and understand their lives as Christians.

5. Adoration. As the group grows together, there should be an increasing amount of time spent in prayer and praise. This accomplishes two things:

● It helps students begin to feel comfortable talking about spiritual matters and praying together, a dimension that becomes increasingly important as they grow into more leadership/*Develop Level*-type roles.

- It helps them to move into the *Disciple Level* of commitment because they practice the discipline of worship and prayer.

Getting Started

In an attempt to develop a small group program for our ministry that would incorporate all of the five components of effective small groups, one youth program I worked with created a program that we called (in a stroke of magnificent creativity) Small Groups! In the interest of building a program that would best meet the needs of our group, the Small Group program had three basic agendas.

- We needed a small group program for our younger teens, a program that did not involve coed groups. For the junior high kids, especially the guys, we felt this would provide an environment more conducive to honest sharing.

- We needed a small group program that would not require *Disciple Level* commitment, a program in which there were few requirements other than consistent attendance. Most of our young junior highers were not *Disciple Level* yet.

- We needed to provide an arena in which our *Develop* and *Multiplier Level* youth could begin to exercise and sharpen ministry skills. By leading these small groups, they were able to test their abilities to deal with Scripture, nurture younger Christians, and take spiritual responsibility for their own peers.

The program designed to meet the needs was a small group program open to junior and senior high school students, small groups that would be segregated according to sex. We decided to use this formula for group makeup because we knew that, to really develop a group in which junior high students would feel open to share, the groups should be set up on a same-sex basis.

In promoting Small Groups, there was an initial mailing to all of our youth giving a fairly clear description of the program (see page 96, which is a slightly revised version of our actual handout). The one and only requirement for participants was consistent attendance. In the information we were careful to stipulate that Small Groups would involve a 13-week commitment. It's important to make clear that the students are not being asked to commit the rest of their natural lives to the Small Group. Without that assurance, some kids who might otherwise get involved would assess the cost and risk of commitment as being too high.

In signing up for Small Group, students could note their choices in

WANTED: LIFELINES OF LOVE

Over the last year we have heard more and more people share that they would like to see us add one thing to our UMYF program that we really don't have. People have shared that even though they are enjoying the weekly Bible studies at Cornerstone and that it's really neat to have all those people up in the Teen Room on Sunday nights when we have Breakaway, there still isn't any opportunity during the week for people to *get together and just share.* If you try to do that on Wednesday night after Bible Study, you flunk a test the next day, and if you try to do that on Sunday night before Breakaway you're liable to get a Ping-Pong ball hit down your throat.

So.......Last year we started trying to build some *Lifelines of Love,* some groups for good, honest sharing. And that was the beginning of our SMALL GROUP program.

A SMALL GROUP IS: a group of friends who meet together on a weekly basis, share their lives (the good and the bad), and pray for each other. It is led by one of our older UMYF members and the group agrees to meet for at least 13 weeks together.

A SMALL GROUP IS NOT: another Bible study, a gossip committee, or just a group of guys to hang around with. You are making a commitment to those in your group to try and be there every week for 13 weeks, and take part in the group.

If you think you may be interested in a SMALL GROUP, fill in the blanks and *turn it in to Duffy before Jan. 9.* You will be assigned to a group on the basis of your sex, which day you can meet, and other secret factors.

- -

I'm interested in being in a **SMALL GROUP:**

Name _____

Male   Female (circle one)   Grade _____   Phone _____

Best day for me to meet:

| Mon. | Tues. | Wed. | Thur. | Fri. | Sat. |

(Circle one)

I'd like _____to be in my group with me.

three particular areas: (1) group leader; (2) one best friend who would definitely be in their group; and (3) what day of the week they would like to meet. While we did not want to put best-friend cliques together, we knew that this choice, assuring them of at least one good friend in their group, would defuse some of their fears about signing up.

Leadership for these groups was provided by some of the *Develop* and *Multiplier Level* students in our program. These students were recruited by the youth leader in a low-key, non-democratic way! Small Group leaders met once a month for training, sharing, and trouble-shooting.

Leaders were instructed that their role was not to give a weekly Bible study. (We didn't feel we could expect them to offer a Bible study every week unless we provided more adult leadership and supervision.) Rather, their role was to lead weekly "people-studies" based on the Bible. In other words, their task was to encourage students to share about their own lives, but center their sharing on one or two particular Bible verses.

"The Permanent Press"

For example, a Small Group leader might use the following text as the focus verse: "Not that I have already obtained it, or have already become perfect, but I press on in order that I may lay hold of that for which also I was laid hold of by Christ Jesus. Brethren, I do not regard myself as having laid hold of it yet; but one thing I do: forgetting what lies behind and reaching forward to what lies ahead, I press on toward the goal for the prize of the upward call of God in Christ Jesus" (Philippians 3:12-14).

Based on that verse, the Small Group leader might give these instructions to the group: "Paul's emphasis here is about being consistent in your walk with Christ. It's almost like you could entitle this passage 'The Permanent Press.' But let's think about our own spiritual lives. I just wonder, if washing instructions came with your spiritual life, what kind of instructions would be given? Here are some options:

- *Permanent press* — ready to wear
- *Dry clean only* — excessive stretching may rip seams
- *Delicate* — suited for lukewarm handling
- *Wash carefully* — apt to fade
- *Hang dry only* — may shrink in intense heat

"I'd like you guys to use this as a springboard and share with the group why one of those sets of instructions might come with your spiritual life."

Without going into the dynamics of small groups, this gives some idea of the kind of material that was used in Small Group. Sometimes students prepared their own materials, but they were free to get materials from the youth office or from volunteers. Essentially, it was the job of the adult leadership to facilitate the leadership ministry of our students.

One of the ways this adult "oversight" was built in was by assigning one adult volunteer to each Small Group leader as a Small Group Overseer. Using a contact sheet (example on the following page) these Overseers were responsible for phoning their Small Group leaders once a week to encourage them, to see if they had special concerns or needs, and to build in some accountability.

COVENANT GROUPS: FOR COMMITTED STUDENTS

We developed a second type of small group ministry that was designed particularly for students at the *Disciple Level,* a ministry we called Covenant Group. Covenant Group was a coed small group that involved quite a bit more commitment than Small Group, and was open only to high school students.

The basic requirements of the program were simple, but important. Students who were unfaithful to the terms of the covenant were encouraged to either become more faithful or withdraw until such time as they could genuinely fulfill the terms of the agreement. (See sample Covenant agreement on page 100.) To make sure that Covenant Group did not become some sort of "spiritual green berets," we required all CG members to consistently attend our weekly Bible study, Cornerstone, and our weekly *Come Level* meeting, Breakaway.

Covenant Group members were also required to keep a journal or diary of their devotional thoughts and insights. This was done (a) to insure that they were building a pattern of daily devotions, and (b) because it was important for them to give some reflection about what God was doing in their lives so that they would have something significant to share when they came to a weekly Tuesday morning meeting of the group.

This helped us to keep sharing to the point, and it limited the number of prayer requests related to diseases and sicknesses of

CONTACT SHEET

Small Group Overseer _____
(your name)

Group Members _____

Small Group
Leader(s)   _____ _____ _____

_____ _____ _____

Leader's Name	Date Contacted	Report	Needs	Comment

COVENANT GROUP

Covenant *(Kuv'e-nant)*, n. a written agreement; a deed; a free promise of God's blessing; a solemn agreement of fellowship and faith between members of a church.

YOU ARE INVITED to be part of an experiment in spiritual adventure . . . not something for everybody . . . a challenge . . . an exercise in commitment and faith . . . a solemn agreement of fellowship and faith between members of Christ's body!

The **COVENANT GROUP** is simply a group of people who are willing to make a 13-week agreement or covenant with each other that they will genuinely seek to (a) grow in their relationships with Christ individually, and (b) grow in their relationships with each other as a group. In the last year there have been a number in our UMYF who point to the Covenant Group as the most meaningful experience they have had in their walks with Christ.

The Covenant Group *IS NOT* some kind of "spiritual Green Berets" or "Superheroes" — it is a group of people serious about making a 13-week commitment to maintain certain disciplines. Basically, those in the Covenant Group are 9th- through 12th-graders who are willing to make a "solemn agreement" to:

(1) Consistently attend *CORNERSTONE and BREAKAWAY* each week. In addition, Covenanters must attend a special retreat (no cost to you) on May 11-12.

(2) Attend a weekly Tuesday morning breakfast at church before school beginning at 6:30. The first breakfast will be on Tuesday morning, January 24. You will be expected to be at the breakfast consistently and *ON TIME* (please note this).

(3) Practice the discipline of a daily Quiet Time *and* bring with you each Tuesday morning an entry into a Quiet Time Diary or personal spiritual journal to be kept during the 13 weeks.

(4) Enroll in the "Onward Bound" Program. Information available from Youth Office.

If you wish to make such a commitment or covenant, sign here and return this entire sheet to Duffy. It will be returned to you at our first prayer and sharing breakfast on Tuesday morning, January 24, 6:30.

NAME

relatives. (It is, of course, much easier for kids to make those kinds of requests than to share their own struggles and needs.)

The Covenant Group met once a week for breakfast and sharing together. Eating the breakfast may have been the toughest requirement of all! The cold cereal and overdone buns made a breakfast that only the spiritually hearty would tolerate. But the sharing and prayer were warm and precious. Students would work their way around the table, reading their journals, some sharing an insight from Scripture, another asking for prayer, and another talking about something he had learned from a Christian book he was reading through for Onward Bound. Many times there were tears. Many times laughter. Always there was love, acceptance, honest sharing, and a genuine experience of the "fellowship of the Holy Spirit."

At the completion of the 13-week Covenant agreement, students could either "reenlist" or they could withdraw without any sense of guilt or pressure. Always, at the end of our 13 weeks, we celebrated our group and our experience with a one-night retreat that was low-budget, low-key, and very low-programming.

This retreat allowed the group time for reflection on our common and individual experiences. I've seen huge crowds at *Come Level* events, hilarious skits, and super ski weekends, but I can say without question that these one-night retreats were some of the most meaningful hours of youth ministry I've known.

The final element of Covenant Group in which students were required to take part was Onward Bound.

ONWARD BOUND:
A PROGRAM OF PERSONAL GROWTH
AND DISCIPLESHIP

Sally is a junior in high school. Two years ago at our winter retreat, Sally made a very genuine and life-changing decision to be a follower of Jesus Christ. In a lot of ways, she's a youth worker's dream. She's active in our program. She reaches out to her friends at school. Her daily time in the Word is at a level of consistency that I had reached by my second year of seminary!

Sally's problem is that she is very weak in the area of personal management. She arrives late to meetings, if she remembers to come at all, and she is generally undependable. Her grades have been slipping at school, and at home her room has been investigated by the EPA as a possible site for Superfund clean-up. Not only has all of this disorganization begun to affect her relationships with parents and friends, it's beginning to bother Sally and affect the way she thinks about herself.

Five years ago, I would have dealt with Sally in one of two equally unproductive ways:

1. *"Sally is a typical teenager."* I would have shrugged my shoulders and shaken my head, having resigned myself to the fact that "kids are kids" and that as long as Sally wasn't on drugs or sexually involved with some guy, then I was doing my job. My prayer for Sally would have been that "she will grow up and act like an adult." (It never occurred to me then that it is that attitude that has produced so many adults who act like teenagers!) I really never thought of Sally's "decision to be a follower of Christ" as being something that would reach into the mundane affairs of personal management.

2. *"Sally needs to be reconverted."* I might have assumed that Sally "just isn't serious about the Lord. If, after all, she were really sold out to Jesus, she would be dealing with these problem areas." Somehow, maybe we were wrong about Sally's decision on that winter retreat. I might have dealt with Sally by assuming that she had fallen away from her commitment to Christ, or that perhaps her conversion just wasn't real enough or deep enough.

Two Common Mistakes

Each of these approaches to Sally's growing pains represents two very common errors related to the spiritual growth of teenagers.

1. We ignore the fact that spiritual growth is practical. Samuel Chadwick, a godly preacher of the eighteenth century, reportedly used to pray, "Lord, make us intensely spiritual, thoroughly practical, and perfectly natural." He understood that holiness is not an obsolete monastic discipline that wouldn't play out in daily life. Biblical holiness should affect every dimension of life, and so should it be in the lives of our youth. We have mistakenly believed or implied that having sex too soon is a spiritual problem, but that getting to an appointment too late is not.

The Apostle Paul said, "I decided to know nothing among you except Christ and Him crucified" (1 Corinthians 2:2, RSV), but he went on to speak in that same letter about widely ranging issues of practical lifestyle. I was encouraging Sally to be intensely spiritual. I'm not sure I knew how to help her make holiness thoroughly practical.

2. We forget that spiritual growth is a process. With all of our talk about the difference that Christ can make in a student's life, we've forgotten that spiritual growth takes time. I like to remind kids of God's words in Deuteronomy 7:22-23 that "the Lord your God will clear away these nations before you little by little; you will not be able to put an end to them quickly, lest the wild beasts grow too numerous for you" (NASB). Spiritual growth is a process of attacking one beast at a time.

Like so many Christian teenagers in our youth groups, Sally did not need to be "reconverted" (whatever that means). Sally was tuned to the right channel, but to make the image still clearer, she needed some fine-tuning. Unfortunately, youth ministry in most churches seems to be geared to channel-changing. We have not been very effective with fine-tuning.

The Fine Art of Fine-Tuning

Fine-tuning is a one-to-one process. In trying to meet Sally's needs, most of us might initiate a series of Bible studies about time management or "doing all things heartily, as serving God and not men" (based on Colossians 3:23), and that's great. But what about John who is just as interested in spiritual growth as Sally, but the beast he needs to attack is a bad relationship with his sister? And then there's Steve who is a fantastic kid, really loves the Lord, but can't seem to work out his relationship with his parents. The problem with fine-tuning is that it varies for each receiver. It is not a group activity. We need to find a way to meet the unique fine-tuning needs of each of the youth in our program.

Fine-tuning takes time. The reason that we don't give more attention to this sort of ministry is that it is very time-consuming. Fine-tuning takes careful listening. Trying to do this kind of ministry without the aid of a volunteer team is impossible except for the smallest of programs. To help the Sallys and Steves and Johns deal with their problems requires accountability. It is not enough to suggest strategies of dealing with these issues. There need to be occasions for frequent "checking-in."

Fine-tuning takes creativity. It's not so hard to keep Sally away from drugs; there's material available. There are books and studies to use. A lot of the work has been done. As I began to work with some of these areas of fine-tuning, I realized that this would be more difficult. Publishers don't sense as broad a market for the fine-tuning

103

issues, so there is less material. Moreover, I learned quickly that if we were going to effect a change in behavior, we were going to have to do more than assign books to read or verses to memorize. That demands creativity.

Onward Bound

With all of these factors in mind, we developed a program of personal growth and discipleship. Based on Paul's statements in Philippians 3:12-14, we used this program to stress the ongoing process of spiritual growth and commitment for the long haul. This program, Onward Bound, was open to any students interested in a growth plan that would be personally tailored to meet their needs. The students were told up front that it would be time-consuming, and that they were expected to make and keep a 13-week commitment to the program. (See page 105 for a sample promotional piece.)

Phase one: Evaluation We used a three-phase strategy with each youth who signed on. Phase One involved *evaluation*. The first step was to help each student explore and consider areas in which he or she needed to grow. This was done using four sources of input:

• *Taylor-Johnson temperament analysis.* All Onward Bound participants were given this rather simple test to help them get a self-portrait of their temperament. This particular instrument evaluates traits like Nervous versus Composed, Active-Social versus Quiet, Depressive versus Light-hearted, Hostile versus Tolerant, Self-Disciplined versus Impulsive, etc. While this is a helpful tool, the particular instrument used is not that important. Students who enrolled in the program the second year were given a "Spiritual Life Check-up" prepared by Dennis Wayman (see *Leadership,* Fall, 1983) which was equally helpful.

• *Parental evaluation forms.* The parents of each student were sent a short letter, signed by the student, asking for their honest input about various elements of the student's personal habits (use of free time, accepting responsibility around the house, keeping room acceptable, contributing to unity and health of the family, etc.). The letter made it clear that these responses would be shared with the students. (See the sample on pages 106 and 107.)

• *Personal interview.* This interview provided two final sources of input: (1) The students were given the results of both their Taylor-Johnson analyses and the parental evaluation forms and asked where they felt they needed work; (2) As the youth minister, I gave them

ONWARD BOUND

A PROGRAM OF PERSONAL GROWTH AND DISCIPLESHIP

. . . .

If you are a person committed to Jesus Christ . . . committed to growth . . . committed to being stretched by God's Word and God's Spirit . . . open to "pressing on" in your walk with Christ, *then,* ONWARD BOUND *is for you!*

"I do not claim that I have already become perfect. I press on for the prize of the upward call of God in Christ Jesus. Of course, my brothers, I really do not think that I have made it; the one thing I do, however, is to forget what is behind me and do my best to reach what is ahead."

—Paul (Philippians 3:12-14)

What is Onward Bound?—Onward Bound is a totally new program for the UMYF, but the concept is as old as Christianity. Onward Bound is a program designed to meet the needs of the many in our fellowship who are eager and ready to chart a course of personal Christian growth for themselves, that will help them to focus specifically on some areas in which they personally need to grow.

. . . .

Who can take part in the Onward Bound program?—The Onward Bound program is open to every member of our UMYF Fellowship, but that doesn't mean everybody should do it. There are some in our group who, in addition to the regular Bible studies, etc., we have each week at Cornerstone and Sunday School, desire to get some individual encouragement and guidance for areas that they really want to zero in on. It will require commitment, and some time to meet with your growth partner at least once every week or two.

. . . .

How does it work?—Onward Bound consists of two phases: (1) Evaluation: Finding some areas in which you feel you need to grow; helping each person discover some areas that need work which the person might not even be aware of; spending some time considering your strengths and weaknesses. (2) Focus: Choosing an area to really focus in on; discussing this area with Duffy and your growth partner and determining a growth strategy that will involve Scripture memorization, sharing what you've learned with others, reading some material that may help you work on the area you've chosen, and then putting what you've learned into practice.

. . . .

How do I join?—Just sign your name on the form below, and then make an interview appointment with Duffy *immediately.*

ONWARD BOUND: _____ Phone: _____

105

ONWARD BOUND
Parents' Input Form

Dear Mom/Dad:

Please fill out the evaluation form below as honestly and completely as you can. Your input will help me evaluate points on which I want to focus in my Onward Bound Growth Contract. Duffy will share your input with me, so please be as specific and as honest as you can be. I understand that your comments are made in love, and I know that you understand that I ask for this input so that I can continue to tune up my relationship with my family and my Lord.

Sincerely,

. . . .

■ **FAMILY RELATIONSHIPS**

	Very True	Usually True	Some-times	Not Often
1. I feel that my son/daughter is considerate of the rights and feelings of other family members.				
2. _____ is willing to share himself with other family members.				
3. _____ is willing to assume his share of responsibility in our family by helping around the house.				
4. _____ contributes to the spiritual atmosphere in our household.				

(Parent's Input Form continued)

■ PERSONAL HABITS

	Very True	Usually True	Some-times	Not Often
1. _____ is disciplined in the management of his time.				
2. _____ wastes a lot of time by watching TV or talking on the phone more than I feel he/she should.				
3. _____ seems to be doing his/her best in whatever task he/she undertakes.				
4. _____ does his/her best to keep his/her room clean and presentable(!).				

GENERAL COMMENTS

Are there other areas where you would like to see some work? What do you observe as your son/daughter's greatest strengths? Any other comments or explanation of above answers?

PARENTS: This form is not confidential. I will share the results with your son/daughter. But please return it by mail to Duffy Robbins c/o Wilmore UMC, P.O. Box 68. Thanks for your help.

my evaluation of where they needed to grow.

Phase two: Growth Contract Based on the above information, we moved to phase two: *drawing up a growth contract.* For each student, a personally tailored program of growth was created. (See the sample blank contract on page 109.) This Growth Contract involved at least four categories of focus:

• *Scripture.* Each contract involved some element of Bible study or memorization, or both.

• *Reading.* Students were assigned a book or articles that would give some insight into the area with which they struggled.

• *Practice.* Each student was given some assignment that had to do with actually putting growth goals into some observable behavior. This might involve keeping a log of how many arguments Steve has with his parents in the next two weeks, listing the time, the circumstances, subject, and result of the disagreement. That gave the student a chance to observe his or her behavior more objectively, and it often showed us ways that reconciliation could take place.

• *Sharing.* Each student was assigned some area in which to share his or her goals and how each was working to grow through personal struggles. A student might share with his small group one thing learned from each of the chapters in the book he was assigned to read.

Phase three: Accountability During phase three, over the course of the next 13 weeks, each student met with one of the ministry team members semiweekly. These Growth Partners were responsible for seeing that each student was making progress in his or her contract, and even more so, helping students to reflect on what they were learning through their various assignments. These meetings usually lasted an hour-and-a-half, and they were the absolute key to the effectiveness of the strategy.

Signs of Progress

For the first time, we were seeing some real progress in some of the trouble areas that had been so elusive for our kids. They sensed the growth in their own lives and were able to see the practical implications of spirituality on a daily basis. Needless to say, it was helpful to our leaders in that it gave them a format for working with students one-on-one.

An unexpected by-product of the program was the renewed parental support. Parents sensed this was one tangible way we were work-

GROWTH CONTRACT

"I do not claim that I have already become perfect. I press on for the prize of the upward call of God in Christ Jesus. Of course, my brothers, I really do not think that I have made it; the one thing I do, however, is to forget what is behind me and do my best to reach what lies ahead."
— Paul (Philippians 3:12-14)

Date _____

Please complete this growth contract carefully, prayerfully, and completely. This is a covenant, A PROMISE, that to the best of your ability, with God's help, you will complete the contract below. This contract is based on areas of growth that you have pinpointed for special concentration. Be willing to push yourself. Your Growth Partner is taking valuable time to meet with you. Make those meetings count. Try to meet with him/her a minimum of three times, four times if possible.

I, _____, in an effort to "press on for the prize of the upward call of God in Christ Jesus," do solemnly commit myself, with God's help, to grow in the following areas of my life. I understand that I will be held accountable for these goals and that my contract to grow in these areas is not to be taken lightly.

REMEMBER: BE SPECIFIC!!

Goal One: _____

Goal Two: _____

Goal Three: _____

It is **my responsibility** to meet with my growth partner. I will be responsible for setting up meetings on the following days/times:

No. 1 _____ No. 2 _____ No. 3 _____ No. 4 _____

This contract is to be finished by _____ (Date). In order to make progress toward these goals I have stated, I will work in the following growth areas with the assignments listed below:

SCRIPTURE: _____

READING: _____

PRACTICE: _____

SHARING: _____

ing with them to nurture their child. Another unexpected dividend was the increase in reading Christian books. As kids shared how Tim Stafford's book, *The Trouble with Parents,* had been helpful to them, other students wanted to read it. We developed a library out of the youth office.

Warning!

As with any system, the results are only as good as the people running the system. The Growth Partners can make or break the whole idea. Second, it is vital that students be forced to shape very specific growth goals going into phase three. It's too easy to say, "I want to be more of a blessing to my family." Accountability is almost impossible with a goal like that. Ed and Bobbie Reeds' criteria (*Creative Bible Learning for Youth,* Gospel Light/ICL) for choosing good objectives are helpful here. Students should be encouraged to use goals that are measurable (one can know if one has reached them), reachable (it is possible to accomplish this in 13 weeks), and ownable (it is the student's goal and not what the student thinks I want him to choose for a goal).

A final caution is that spiritual growth doesn't come through programs; it comes through people. Onward Bound is simply a structure designed to meet a need. A different need might call for a completely different structure or for an adaptation of the one given here. The key is to find some means of encouraging our students to grow progressively into the image of Christ.

Sally doesn't need to be ignored until she has a drastic breakdown. Nor does she need to be nagged into reconversion so that *this* time she can really, really, really get serious about Jesus. Like most growing things, Sally needs nurture, care, pruning, and the right environment.

A Vision or a Dream?

It's been almost eight years since I first typed out much of the material in this book, as it was originally published under the title *Programming to Build Disciples*. Since that time, God has granted me the thrill of hearing from youth workers all over the world who have made use of the principles and programs suggested in these pages. Nothing gets me more excited than speaking at a youth ministry convention in New Zealand and being approached by some "kiwi" youth worker who tells me how these concepts have shaped his ministry! One of the most genuine privileges of my life has been to indirectly impact the lives of teenagers around the world, most of whom I will not meet until heaven.

At the same time, I well realize that writing a book about youth ministry is easier than actually doing youth ministry. Particularly if you're just starting out in youth work, it seems a bit intimidating. How do I start? Where should I go? When can I quit? It's easy to wonder if we really can make a difference.

If you're feeling that kind of bewilderment at the end of this book, I hope you will be as encouraged as I was by the following letter. It was written by one of my former volunteer youth leaders who eventually went on to seminary and, after graduation, began to do his own ministry with kids.

I apologize for printing a personal letter sent to me. It's not meant to be boastful. (It's just that letters written to other people are not normally delivered to my office, so I don't really have ready access to those documents.) My lackluster athletic career has never shown a need for a trophy case at our house. It doesn't take that much space to display a varsity letter in Band. But the following letter is one of the "trophies" that I am eager to display, because it demonstrates quite clearly that a ministry of multiplication works, and that we CAN impact the life of teenagers with the Gospel of Christ.

> I think one of the biggest problems I have in ministry today is that I don't take enough time to reflect on my ministry; I just do ministry. This can be a great mistake because if you are headed in the wrong direction, it doesn't take long to get lost. But you're not the only one lost, you have taken a number of teens with you. We all stand around saying, "What are we doing here?"
>
> Duffy, I feel like I owe you much of my success in ministry. How could I disciple teens if you had not shown me the need? I'm sure I would be burnt out by now. But, because of what you've taught, my heart burns within to continue to share Christ with teens.
>
> I remember starting in Frankfort [KY] with two teens. Two teens! Faithfully I met with them every Wednesday for Bible study. Then, soon there were five teens. I got them all involved with personal growth contracts through our Onward Bound program. They grew in Christ weekly and I could see Christ in them. They soon began to reach out to others. They were sharing their faith with their friends! UMYF [United Methodist Youth Fellowship] began to grow! My last UMFY meeting had 55 teens. And those teens loved Jesus. I never once did evangelism. The teens did it all. I helped in the discipleship process. My time was limited (I was part-time) and they brought teens in faster than I could deal with them. I believe Onward Bound is one of the most important tools of youth ministry that I have ever found. It makes Covenant Group and Small Groups possible, and most important of all, it makes growth possible. . . .
>
> Looking back in my five years in Frankfort I saw God take teens and make them men and women of God. One is serving as a full-time youth minister. One starts seminary next year to become a full-time youth minister. One is at college studying to be a youth minister.
>
> One is at the University of Kentucky and then plans to attend seminary to prepare for youth ministry. She also served in a camp in Oregon this past summer. What a miracle of God!

When I met her she didn't know who God was! Through Onward Bound she came to know God intimately (four years in the Onward Bound program).

One of my teens went overseas in mission work after graduation. One got involved in Christian music (I taught him how to play guitar), and now he travels with a Christian rock group. (He's much better than I ever dreamed of being.)

Brother, I just wanted to thank you for sharing so much with me. I know God has you right where He wants you. I'm sure you miss being out on the front lines with your own youth group, but just through your time with me, at least four more have been sent to the front lines. Keep sending them out, Duff!

Take care brother,

Frank

MISSION POSSIBLE

The quick answers never seem to work very well in youth ministry. Experience teaches most of us that lesson sooner or later. But, even more so, my experience has taught me that the most fitting answer, or the most practical program, will accomplish very little if it isn't infused with the Spirit of God. Anyone who attempts to use these ideas without spending some serious time on his or her knees is probably going to find them as dry and lifeless as last year's bird's nest!

Even with fervent and consistent prayer, though, there are times when youth ministry can be woefully frustrating. For that reason, I'd like to close this book with an excerpt from the *Addresses and Papers of John R. Mott* (yes, it is a catchy title!). Mott, of course, was one of the pioneers of the Student Christian Movement that led hundreds of men and women to the mission field around the turn of this century. Though his own mission work was largely in China, his impact was, quite literally, worldwide. Near the end of his life, Mott wrote the following lines in his journal:

As I lay thinking this afternoon I asked myself, "What would I do if I had my life to live over again?" I would give vastly more emphasis and concentration upon schoolboys. This vision-forming period when the character and aims of life is shaped is of primary and central importance. For instance, if asked what I would do in China, I would pick 100 of the strongest men and women of the West and ask them to give themselves entirely to the service of the high school boys and girls in the government schools of that country.

The first time I read that quote, I was struck almost simultaneously with two thoughts that have consistently challenged me. To begin with, I was impressed with how different might the world be today if John R. Mott had followed through on that vision earlier in his life. How might history have been radically changed? How different our current world situation might be if Mott had given himself "entirely" to the student population of China in the early 1900s. After all, that is the generation that has leadership in that massive nation even today. But, of course, I was immediately confronted with the realization that now the opportunity has passed. It's too late for John R. Mott. That's when I was confronted with this second thought: *It's not too late for us!* We can still make a difference. By the power of God, we can even change history.

For my money, that's why youth ministry is so exciting. That's why I'm so encouraged that there are people willing to "give themselves entirely to the service of the high school boys and girls" of this country.

With the conclusion of this book, I want to encourage my brothers and sisters in youth ministry to take full advantage of our opportunity now. How tragic that, in years to come, we might look back like Mott with all his accomplishments, and lament that, because we had been under-committed to youth ministry, we had overlooked great opportunity for the Gospel. I hope and pray that we'll continue to be haunted and challenged by that vision.

Materials for Student Growth

Bergan, Jacqueline Syrup and Schwan, S. Marie. *Forgiveness, A Guide for Prayer,* Saint Mary's Press, 1985.

_____. *Birth, A Guide for Prayer,* Saint Mary's Press, 1985.

_____. *Surrender, A Guide for Prayer,* Saint Mary's Press, 1986.

_____. *Freedom, A Guide for Prayer,* Saint Mary's Press, 1986.
This series wouldn't work for every kid, but this Roman Catholic resource looks at some of the spiritual disciplines that aren't addressed in more popular curriculums. Could be used in one-on-one and small group settings with more mature Christian students.

Bray, Marian Flandrick, *Stepping Over Stones,* Augsburg Publishing House, 1988.
This book uses stories to help kids think about some of the problems of being a teenager. Could be used with individual students or as a resource for discussion.

Burns, Jim. *Handling Your Hormones,* Merit Books, 1984.
Still one of the most widely-read books in the area of sex and dating. Beyond Jim Burn's own warm personality and disarming style, this book offers frank discussions of some of the issues not addressed as directly in some of the other books of this type.

Burns, Ridge with Becchetti, Noel. *The Complete Student Missions Handbook,* Youth Specialties, 1990.
One of the best books on the market for those who are exploring ways to involve their students in some sort of missions outreach.

Good information on various inexpensive, close-to-home mission projects as well.

Campbell, Stan. *BibleLog Thru-the-Bible Series,* Victor Books, 1988. This is Victor's new Bible survey material. It may be the most readable and user-friendly Bible survey curriculum for teenagers on the market. May not want to use this as a steady diet year round, but this can be a good resource when you need it. Could also be used by individual students who really want to get a good overview of Scripture. A leader's guide is available.

Christian, S. Rickly. *Alive (Daily Devotions),* Campus Life Books of Zondervan Publishing House, 1989.
——————. *Alive (2) Daily Devotions,* Campus Life Books of Zondervan Publishing House, 1983, 1990.
Good devotional tools for students. Provides a daily reading and a parallel passage of Scripture. Helpful first quiet time guides.

Clark, Chap. *Next Time I Fall in Love,* Youth Specialties, 1987.
One of the best and most realistic books in a market flooded with books about dating and guy-girl relationships. Kids seem to like this book because it's fun to read, and because it doesn't get too preachy. It also provides a very practical tool that students can use to evaluate their own relationships.

——————. *Leader's Guide for Next Time I Fall in Love,* Youth Specialties, Youth Specialties, 1989.

Coppedge, Allan. *The Biblical Principles of Discipleship,* Francis Asbury Press, 1989.
Not really written with youth ministry in mind, but still a sound in-depth, perhaps slightly more academic, look at the ministry of disciple-making.

Cosgrove, Francis M., Jr. *Essentials of Discipleship,* Navpress, 1980.
Good book to use for leadership training. Will have to be adapted for youth ministry situations.

Davis, Ken. *How to Live with Your Parents,* Zondervan Publishing House, 1988.
A great book for kids with practical, readable insights about life with parents. Very good.

——————. *I Don't Remember Dropping the Skunk But I Do*

Bibliography

Remember Trying to Breathe, Zondervan Publishing House, 1990. A great book from outstanding communicator, Ken Davis. Students will enjoy this book and they will benefit from reading it.

Dockrey, Karen. *Dating, Making Your Own Choices,* Broadman Press, 1987.

Eschner, Kathleen Hamilton and Nelson, Nancy G. *Drugs, God & Me,* Group Books, 1988.

Fields, Doug and Temple, Todd. *Creative Dating,* Oliver-Nelson Books, 1986.
This book for teenagers is more than just a lot of fun. It is that, to be sure, but it is also one of the few books on the market that goes beyond telling kids what not to do on dates, and gives them some great ideas about what they can do on dates.

Fields, Doug. *How Not To Be a Goon,* Regal Books, 1986.
With a sense of humor and faithfulness to biblical truth, Doug Fields provide here an excellent resource for students who are dealing with questions of peer pressure, fitting in, and living out the Christian life without being terminally weird.

_____. *Creative Times with God,* Harvest House Publishers, 1988.
Excellent. Can be used as a resource for youth workers or for individual students. Gives students creative ways of deepening their relationship with God. Good stuff!

Fishel, Kent M. and Rayls, John W. *Cornerstones: Believing the Bible,* Zondervan Publishing House, 1987.
A good resource that can be used with either one-on-one or small group discipleship.

Fleischmann, Paul (Editor). *Discipleship the Young Person,* Here's Life Publishers, Inc., 1985.
A compendium of articles that draw from youth workers all over the country. The nature of the format makes it tough for the chapters to have much depth, but this is an excellent book to use with volunteer leaders. The brevity of the articles also makes this a good resource if you are looking for an article that addresses a particular issue in discipling teenagers.

Goddard, Hule and Acevodo, Jorge. *The Heart of Youth Ministry,* Bristol Books, 1989.

This book is the kind of book that helps you check the pulse of your own heart for youth ministry. A great book to recommend to volunteers who need to get pumped up and refocused. Very down-to-earth. Both of these authors have spent years in the trenches.

Gunn, Robin Rones. *Summer Promise,* Focus on the Family Publishing, 1988.
Fiction. Well done. Addresses normal teenage issues of love, sex, and independence. Would probably work best with girls.

Hanks, Jr., Billie and Shell, William A. (Editors). *Discipleship,* Zondervan Publishing House, 1981.
This book describes itself as the best writings from the most experienced disciple makers, and that's a fair description. This is an excellent resource for giving adult leaders a vision for discipleship.

Jackson, James W. *What'cha Gonna Do with What'cha Got?,* David C. Cook Publishing Company, 1987.
One of the few curriculums on the market that addresses the issue of money. Good, thoughtful learner-centered materials.

Jones, Larry. *Practice to Win,* Tyndale House Publishers, Inc., 1982.
This is a fairly light devotional help with emphasis on illustrations from athletics. Could be used with individual students who are really into sports.

Keiser, Fred. *Good News Q's,* Youth Specialties, 1988.
This book leaves readers with more questions than answers, but sometimes it's in asking the questions that we really come up with answers we can hold on to. *Good News Q's* would make a great devotional resource for an individual student, or a good discussion resource for small group sessions. The book works through the gospel narrative and simply poses questions based on the text. Also, this book makes a good tool for helping kids learn inductive Bible study.

Kuhne, Gary W. *The Dynamics of Discipleship Training,* Zondervan Publishing House, 1978.
Good book to use for training leaders for a discipleship ministry. Will have to be adapted for youth ministry situations.

Kuniholm, Whitney. *John: A Daily Dialogue with God,* Harold Shaw Publishers, 1982.

This book is a personal Bible study guide with 65 studies and readings. It's a good resource for students who are looking for serious Bible study and devotional material that they can use on their own.

Lawhead, Steve. *Rock of This Age,* InterVarsity Press, 1987.
Lawhead's book is great because it is written by someone who is obviously a fan of rock music. A sane, balanced look at some of the arguments used against listening to any kind of rock music. Again, I wouldn't recommend the book for any but very mature students. However, the resource material will give your teaching in this area a lot more credibility.

Lewis, Gregg and Stafford, Tim. *You Call This a Family?,* Tyndale House Publishers, Inc., 1986.
This is a collection of articles from the pages of *Campus Life* magazine. I've used this with individual students who are working through family problems. It's well-written, helpful, and students find the short chapters easy to read.

Lutes, Chris. *What Teenagers Are Saying About Drugs & Alcohol,* Campus Life Books of Zondervan Publishing House, 1987, 1990.

Lynn, David and Yaconelli, Mike. *Teaching the Truth about Sex,* Youth Specialties, 1990.
A great resource if you plan to teach your youth group about sex. There are hand-outs, role-plays, discussion starters, and lots of other learning strategies here. One unique component of this curriculum is the parental involvement material that comes along with each lesson.

McNabb, Bill and Mabry, Steven. *Teaching the Bible Creatively,* Youth Specialties/Zondervan Publishing House, 1990.
McNabb and Mabry give us here a concise and fun-to-read resource for helping leaders prepare Bible studies for teenagers. Good illustrations and lots of ideas. Would be a great training tool for adult leaders.

Moore, Waylon B. *Multiplying Disciples,* NavPress, 1981.
This book is a New Testament study of discipleship. Probably not the book to use with students or leaders directly, but a very good book for background information.

Peters, Dan and Peters, Steve. *Why Knock Rock?*, Bethany House Publishers, 1984.
A good thoughtful look at the issue of rock music. While this is not the kind of book that is going to turn your head-bangers into Sandi Patti fans, it does offer some good thoughts for teaching your students to use discernment in the area of music.

Rabey, Steve. *Rock the Planet*, Zondervan Publishing House, 1989.
A unique devotional resource for teenagers. Each one page chapter includes a story, a vignette or a reflection from musicians and speakers popular among teenagers as well as some biblical reference. A good idea, and well done.

Robbins, Duffy. *Have I Got News for You*, Graded Press, 1988.
This is a curriculum designed to train students to share their faith. The book itself looks kind of ugly, but youth workers have found the material helpful. There is both a student book and a leader's guide.

_____. *The Ministry of Nurture*, Youth Specialities/Zondervan Publishing House, 1990.
A thorough and practical guide for leaders who want to help their students grow spiritually. Includes several resources, including a Spiritual Life Inventory that has been very helpful.

Sciacca, Fran and Jill. *Desperately Seeking Perfect Family*, World Wide Publications, 1987.
Great small group material for dealing with family relationships.

Smith, Michael W. with Ridenour, Fritz. *Old Enough to Know*, Contempo Books, 1987.
Because of Michael W. Smith's popularity as a Christian musician, some students might be willing to read this book when they wouldn't normally sit down to read a Christian book. The book hits on a lot of the basic issues of being a teenager and being a teenage Christian.

Southern, Randy. *It Came From the Media*, Victor Books, 1989.
An excellent resource for looking with teenagers at the issue of media influence. User-friendly and learner-centered.

Stone, J. David and Keefauver, Larry. *Friend to Friend*, Group Books, 1983.

Bibliography

This book is designed to help teenagers as they counsel with their peers who have problems. Some have criticized as being far too simplistic, but it is probably a realistic effort in terms of trying to give kids some practical handles for helping their friends.

Tirabassi, Becky with Lewis, Gregg. *Just One Victory*, Campus Life Books, Tyndale House Publishers, 1987.
An honest, very readable account of Becky Tirabassi's struggle as a teenage alcoholic. Kids will read this book, and they will take it seriously.

_____. *The Life of the Party*, Campus Life Books of Zondervan Publishing House, 1987, 1990.
Honestly addresses the issue of teenage drinking. Well-written for the teenage audience.

_____. *My Daily Partner*, Tyndale House, 1986.
This book comes in a notebook format. It's a practical tool to help students really dig in to a consistent devotional life. For the right student, this is a great help.

_____. *Quietimes*, Tyndale House, 1986.
Quiet time guide for students. Well-written. The author speaks frequently to students in this area and knows well how to inspire and instruct.